PARENTING
without
PERFECTION

PARENTING
without
PERFECTION

BEING A KINGDOM INFLUENCE IN A TOXIC WORLD

DAVID JOHN SEEL, JR.

NAVPRESS
BRINGING TRUTH TO LIFE
P.O. Box 35001, Colorado Springs, Colorado 80935

OUR GUARANTEE TO YOU

We believe so strongly in the message of our books that we are making this quality guarantee to you. If for any reason you are disappointed with the content of this book, return the title page to us with your name and address and we will refund to you the list price of the book. To help us serve you better, please briefly describe why you were disappointed. Mail your refund request to: NavPress, P.O. Box 35002, Colorado Springs, CO 80935.

The Navigators is an international Christian organization. Our mission is to reach, disciple, and equip people to know Christ and to make Him known through successive generations. We envision multitudes of diverse people in the United States and every other nation who have a passionate love for Christ, live a lifestyle of sharing Christ's love, and multiply spiritual laborers among those without Christ.

NavPress is the publishing ministry of The Navigators. NavPress publications help believers learn biblical truth and apply what they learn to their lives and ministries. Our mission is to stimulate spiritual formation among our readers.

Library of Congress Catalog Card Number: 00-028273
ISBN 1-57683-200-7

Cover Photo by Jeff Cadge
Cover design by Jennifer Mahalik
Creative Team: Amy Boucher Pye, Lori Mitchell, Tim Howard, Vickie Howard

Some of the anecdotal illustrations in this book are true to life and are included with the permission of the persons involved. All other illustrations are composites of real situations, and any resemblance to people living or dead is coincidental.

Unless otherwise identified, all Scripture quotations in this publication are taken from the *Holy Bible: New International Version* ® (NIV®). Copyright © 1973, 1978, 1984 by International Bible Society. Used by permission of Zondervan Publishing House. All rights reserved. Other versions used include: *The Message: New Testament with Psalms and Proverbs* by Eugene H. Peterson, copyright ©1993, 1994, 1995, used by permission of NavPress Publishing Group; the *New King James Version* (NKJV), copyright © 1979, 1980, 1982, 1990, Thomas Nelson Inc., Publishers; and the *King James Version* (KJV).

Seel, David J. (David John), 1925-
    Parenting without perfection: being a kingdom influence in a toxic world /
David John Seel, Jr.
        p. cm.
    Includes bibliographical references.
    ISBN 1-57683-200-7 (pbk.)
        1. Parenting—Religious aspects—Christianity. I. Title.
BV4529 .S42 2000
248.8'45—dc21

Printed in the United States of America

1 2 3 4 5 6 7 8 9 10 / 04 03 02 01 00

To Kathryn
A daily reminder of God's love and grace

"The LORD does not look at the things man looks at. Man looks at the outward appearance, but the LORD looks at the heart."

—1 SAMUEL 16:7

Contents

Acknowledgments

It has been said that "writing is the process by which you explain to yourself what happened to you." I'm quite sure this is right, for writing a book such as this is penning a thinly disguised autobiography. In many ways it is my explanation to myself of the turmoil of the last five years—times of pain and promise, heartache and hope.

It has been a venture of faith, but not one without trusted friends and prayerful partners. I owe much to them, and it is an honor to acknowledge their significant role in the writing of this book. I am thankful for friends such as Wes and Jackie Howard, Tuck and Stacy Bartholomew, Mike and Sarah Dowling, Bob and Jayne Korljan, Gene and Ann Hastings, Richard and Portia White, Chuck and Maria Thomas, Estelle Wilkerson, John Kuebler, Shanon Clark, Jeremy Linzee, Martha MacLeod, Russ Hof, and the entire congregation of Montreat Presbyterian Church.

I am grateful for intellectual mentors such as the late Francis Schaeffer, David Wells, Dallas Willard, Peter Kreeft, Steve Garber, and my former students at The Stony Brook School in Stony Brook, New York.

I owe everything to my family, especially my parents, David and Mary Seel (who purchased the iMac on which this book was written), my in-laws, Dave and Carol Powell, and our three children, Annie, Dave, and Alex.

For the support of Don Simpson at NavPress and competence of Amy Boucher Pye, my editor, I am deeply indebted.

And finally, to my loving wife, Kathryn, who keeps my head grounded in reality and my heart soaring to heaven. It is to her that this book is dedicated—as in her life, I have come to see my Savior's face more clearly.

No Guaranty, No Warranty

PICTURE PERFECT

Pictures may be worth a thousand words, but they don't tell the whole truth. They may depict smiling faces of family members in a Christmas portrait, but they reveal only what we want to divulge and little else. Hidden behind the smiles lie the spiritual and emotional health of those portrayed.

At times we've all sent our own Kodak images of the perfect family enjoying an exotic vacation. But we know better. We can recount the history of the lives and the tears behind the smiles. We see the real picture; we know the truth about our marriages and our children. We have felt the acute pain of divorce, the gut-wrenching fear of custody disputes, the heartrending loss of a prodigal child. We know the reality of raising a family—yes, a Christian family—in today's world.

And yet when we look for help, we sometimes find it hard to relate to the advice we receive. We pick up the books of popular authors who promote parental success and we glimpse their large, happy families on the book jackets. Every shirttail is tucked in and every hair is in place. We can become overawed by the illusion on the cover, even if we know it's just a picture. What's portrayed may seem like a world apart from the reality we live.

But we are not alone, for behind closed doors no "perfect" families exist. This book seeks to open these doors and expose the Christmas images. It addresses the rest of us: the wounded parents who have stopped sending the holiday portraits because the family picture can no longer be taken.

A CALL TO EMBODY JESUS

We all have our histories and their importance, in part, is because they are our own. I have mine. I was raised the son of medical missionaries in a loving if not somewhat enmeshed family. I married, fathered two children, worked for an evangelical campus ministry, graduated from seminary, authored books about the need for reformation and revival in the church, and then experienced my world falling apart. After eighteen years of marriage, I found myself a single parent with custody of two teenage boys. It amazes me that so many people survive broken marriages, because the pain of such an experience is beyond anything Hollywood has ever depicted. It's a living death that won't go away. Who would wish it? But this brokenness happens, and God is especially faithful in those dark hours.

Apart from those times of deep distress, this book neither could have nor would have been written. Any wisdom here has been gained from the trenches. I spent several years teaching at a boarding college preparatory school being immersed in adolescent life. Then for the last two years my studies have focused on youth culture from the vantage point of a college social scientist. I have a blended family now, with two children in college and another in the midst of his adolescent years. Betrayal, divorce, custody battles, remarriage, a blended family, a prodigal child—it's all on my résumé. In the midst of my darkest hours as a parent, I received comfort from David Runcorn's observation:

> There is nothing sadder than a Christian fellowship where every song must be victory, every prayer full of faith, every member always smiling and joyful. It is an exhausting pretense to keep up for long, and it condemns those who

cannot hide from their fears to further pain of failure and inadequacy. It is actually dishonest. It means that we can never offer our tears as well as our smiles, our questions as well as our certainties, our wounds as well as our victories. It means that we are always keeping Christ out of the very places in our lives where we need him most—the place of our darkness, uncertainties, and fears.[1]

This is a book that doesn't hide the wounds. In it I take a realistic look at the challenges and opportunities of parenting adolescents in the context of weakened families and a toxic youth culture. I believe strongly that God has more in mind for parents than striving to produce so-called perfect, well-adjusted children. Rather, parenting is first and foremost a call to embody the incarnational life of Jesus in the midst of our family. To study how this works out in an adolescent's life is the purpose of this book.

WHAT IS CHRISTIAN PARENTING?

In recent years I have come to question some of the common assumptions held by many Christian parents and parenting books. One is that certain choices will isolate one's children from the effects of today's youth culture; another is that following a specific set of guidelines will produce "perfect" children.

But there aren't any failproof recipes, and no secret sauce. Instead, eight questions shape the discussion of parenting in this book. The main one may seem surprising, but greatly affects the way we view our parental role: How does God treat us as children?

The seven other questions follow in the same vein. How is our approach to parenting affected if . . .

1. the goal is children who are apprentices to Jesus?
2. discipleship is understood as more than an intellectual affirmation or outward behavior, but a life lived in, for, and by the resources of the kingdom of God?
3. we come to understand our teenager as a young adult rather than an overgrown child?
4. we respect the self-determining nature of our child and

acknowledge the priority of motivation—the direction
and loves of his or her heart?
5. we acknowledge that youth culture is spiritually toxic
but inescapable by our teenage children?
6. we understand that the choices our teens make outside
our context or control actually influence them the most?
7. we recognize that parenting is a temporary stewardship
with no guarantees?

This book begins by examining these questions while seeking to describe a biblical understanding of the task of Christian
parenting, especially as it relates to adolescent-aged children.

THE CONTEXT OF CHRISTIAN PARENTING

The second part of the book contains a study of contemporary
youth culture—the context of Christian parenting today. What in
academic circles is described as "postmodern" culture in fact
largely describes the beliefs and behavior of youth today. Theirs is
a culture in which God is functionally dead—a spiritually lethal
society that takes no prisoners.

Mary Motley Kalergis interviewed teenagers across the country and highlights the hazards they face: "It takes courage to
accept that our children inhabit a dangerous world, and that,
despite our best efforts, some of them will be wounded or even
killed by their contact with it. The dangers of life will never be
completely eliminated. However, an unrecognized danger is
that, in our zeal to protect our children from life's risks, we evade
the truth about its complexities."[2] Knowing the contours of our
children's world equips us to come to terms with the seriousness
and stakes of the task.

THE PRIORITIES OF CHRISTIAN PARENTING

The book's third section explores ten priorities for Christian parents to consider in best influencing their teenager toward an
authentic life in the kingdom of God. Incarnational in method and
realistic in expectation, these ten points include biblical principles,

the cultural context, and psychological insights. They are not exhaustive but are fundamental to parenting teens as God parents us. The ten priorities for us as parents are:

1. To be apprentices of Jesus
2. To live our life with integrity for that which matters
3. To be students of our teenager's world
4. To advocate our child's constructive interests
5. To establish limits for our teenager based on the objective truth of reality
6. To encourage our teenager to become a passionate seeker of truth
7. To focus on influencing the beliefs, not the behavior, of our teen
8. To respect our child's self-determination
9. To recognize that our teenager's friends and neighborhood will influence his or her heart's direction
10. To pray for our child as our first responsibility

As we will see, parenting adolescents teaches us the requirement of love, of letting go of our children in order to entrust them to God. It is then that we enter the "Golden Age of Parenting," a term one author used to describe parenting teenagers. Unlike what that author probably meant, the golden age is a time when the metal of a parent's spiritual reality is tested, refined, and made as gold.

LEAN HARD

An old Southern expression has been passed down in my family through my grandfather, Alex Batchelor, to my mother, Mary Seel: "Lean hard." These two words direct us to Jesus. The phrase makes little sense to the steady, strong, and secure. But when we're in trouble, when our world has fallen apart, and when we are beside ourselves with anguish, this short saying points us in the right direction.

"Lean hard" is the phrase we can remember when we are waiting up past curfew for our teenage daughter to return. It is what we can think of when countless letters to a prodigal son go unanswered. It is what we can ponder when the police call saying that our child is in their custody. It is what we remember when our questions are met with adolescent silence or when instruction is followed by the teenage disconnect, "Whatever."

"Lean hard" is what we learn as the circumstances of parenting teach us again and again that we are not finally in control of our teenage children. For they are God's gift; a temporary stewardship to teach us to live beyond ourselves. The psalmist writes, "Blessed are those whose strength is in you, who have set their hearts on pilgrimage" (Psalm 84:5). Parenting is a pilgrimage of the heart. Lean hard.

PART ONE

WHAT IS CHRISTIAN PARENTING?

CHAPTER ONE

Empty Promises

TRAINING TIPS

Promises of parental success and sanity are hot today: Dr. Dobson and Dr. Laura fill the airwaves with expert advice; people crowd into seminars on "Taking Control of Your Family" and "Managing Your Teen" by John Rosemond; parents purchase curricula on "Growing Kids God's Way" and visit Christian bookstores for the latest on no-fault child-rearing. How-to manuals abound for the parentally insecure or the overly conscientious.

No doubt, most parents just wing it. But new parents, those with a so-called difficult child, and those whose daughter is skipping school or whose son has joined a group of unapproved friends are more than open to biblical principles, psychological guidance, and helpful hints.

Many parenting books written by both Christian and nonChristian authors assume that if you follow certain parenting principles, communication skills, or psychological insights, then—presto!—your child will turn out just fine. Such claims, however, can be hollow. And the promises of perfection can turn out to be empty.

DISTURBING BEHAVIOR

The teen movie *Disturbing Behavior* (1998) raises an important question of the typical child-rearing book: Just how far are parents

and educators willing to go to have children who respect authority and are motivated academically? In looking at this question the
film focuses on Steve Clark, a high-school senior whose parents
decide to move to an idyllic town on a distant northwest island
after Steve's older brother commits suicide. Steve's parents want the
family to escape the influences of the big city.

As an outsider at Cradle Bay High School, Steve is unfamiliar
with the teen class system. A weed-smoking drughead named
Gavin befriends him and shows him the ropes. CB High, he
explains, has five social groupings: the motorheads, skaters, freaks,
micro-geeks, and at the top, the Blue Ribbons. This final group is
made up of the good kids—those who respect adults, achieve
academically, boost the school spirit, and are community-minded.

As the film unfolds, Steve discovers that parents of the Blue
Ribbons have sent them to a school-sponsored Enlightenment
Seminar. There, without the knowledge of the parents, school, or
the kids themselves, a computer chip is placed in their minds to
assure good behavior. Without the freedom to rebel, the Blue
Ribbons are effectively robots. Nonetheless, the results are impres-
sive. Unlike the drugged-out freaks, these "perfect" teenagers are
the pride of their parents, teachers, and administrators.

Steve is horrified and confronts the smooth-talking Dr. Edgar
Caldicott, the mind-control researcher who oversees the program
for the school. Caldicott retorts, "Steven, there will always be troubled teens. There will always be worried parents. Science is god."

A real turning point comes when Steve's parents sign him up
for the program. "We're here for you no matter what," they
explain. "We want what is best for you. We just want you back."
Steve yells, *"What about what I want?"*

The film may sound far-fetched, but its premise is not as
implausible as might be imagined. The goal of controlling
behavior is paramount in such books as *Parents in Control* by
Gregory Bodenhamer, a former probation officer. This author
teaches parents how to master their children through techniques
used to control prison inmates.[1] In the future, such controlled
results might be achieved through a genetically engineered child
with the compliance profile purchased at a premium.

Perhaps the movie's most obvious parallel today is the juvenile-reform program. Teen Help, for instance, promises to turn the most wayward youth into a "loving, caring, and responsible individual." Parents sign waivers allowing the staff to use extreme forms of behavior-modification techniques on their children, such as Mace, handcuffs, stun guns, and solitary confinement. After nearly two years of Teen Help in an isolated camp on the island of Samoa, nineteen-year-old Joe Medoro said, "What you learn over there is how to manipulate people."[2]

ROBOTS OR IMAGE-BEARERS?

Philosopher Dallas Willard sides with the freaks in *Disturbing Behavior* and warns against parental approaches that control: "In close personal relationships, conformity to another's wishes is not desirable, be it ever so perfect, if it is mindless, purchased at the expense of freedom, and destructive of personality."[3] The possibility of rebellion is the mark of being made in the image of God.

As parents, we are stewards of young people who bear the image of God and whose lives will finally be directed by the choices they make before their Creator. Willard reminds over-controlling parents that "God has paid an awful price to arrange for human self-determination. He obviously places great value on it. It is, after all, the *only* way He can get the kind of personal beings He desires for His eternal purposes."[4]

Yet many people read Proverbs 22:6 as though it were the fine print on a life-insurance policy: "Train a child in the way he should go, and when he is old he will not turn from it." But this verse is better understood alongside Proverbs 19:18: "Discipline your son, for in that there is hope; do not be a willing party to his death." Here the emphasis is on our God-given parental responsibilities of training and disciplining. Clearly, we need to interpret the Bible correctly, and especially Proverbs, the most frequently quoted book for child-rearing.

As biblical scholars Gordon Fee and Douglas Stuart write, "There is no guarantee, of course, that life will always go well for a young person. What Proverbs does say is that, all things being equal, there are basic attitudes and patterns of behavior that will help a person grow into responsible adulthood."[5]

Yet the promises of perfection abound. In *Will My Children Go to Heaven?* Edward Gross suggests that by following his principles, parents can guarantee their children's conversion. He writes, "I will show from Scripture that parents can be sure that their children will be saved and go to heaven."[6]

But the Bible makes no such declarations because parenting is always a two-way street. As author Tedd Tripp reminds us, "You must do all that God has called you to do, but the outcome is more complex than whether you have done the right things in the right way. Your children are responsible for the way they respond to your parenting."[7]

Parenting principles are best learned in the three hardest cases: the strong-willed child, the adolescent, and the prodigal. It is easy to dismiss these children as the exception rather than the norm—we blame our difficulties in parenting on their personalities, hormones, or rebelliousness. But in fact, these children illustrate the fact that no one *can* nor *should* control another human being. Even from the youngest age, our children are self-determining spiritual beings; from their youngest age, we must learn to parent with this in mind.[8]

PUFFED-UP PRONOUNCEMENTS

Much of the success language we find in parenting books is merely marketing hype for pop psychology. These claims may boost sales and even alter behavior within a home, but they provide no assurance for a changed life. And if we examine the books closely, we see that many of the authors are parents who still have young children.

Reality, however, has a way of taking some of the wind out of parents' overly confident sails. Those who have made it through their child's teenage years are much less likely to pronounce, "Do these steps and get this great result." Even such platitudes as "follow God's methods to produce God's child" have a certain hollowness. As we see in the Bible, God's nurturing always leaves room for His children's rebellion.

Puffed-up assumptions of success reflect an ungodly humanism. Child-development expert Judith Harris correctly points out,

The nurture assumption is the product of a culture that has as its motto: "We can overcome." With our dazzling electronic devices, our magical biochemical elixirs, we can overcome nature. Sure, children are born different, but that's no problem. Just put them through this marvelous machine here—step right up, ladies and gentlemen!—and add our special patented mixture of love, limits, time-outs, and educational toys. Voila! A happy, smart, well-adjusted, self-confident person![9]

But ever since Cain and Abel, parenting has neither been so simple nor so "successful."

What happens, then, when the smiles turn to grimaces? How do we react when the how-to steps lead nowhere? As we will see in the next chapter, the three most common responses are fear, denial, and retreat.

CHAPTER TWO

Anxiety Epidemic

"HELP!"

Today, anxiety about parenting preteens and teens is reaching epidemic proportions. "All parents feel an ominous sense—like distant thunder moving closer and closer—that even their child could be caught in the deluge of adolescent dysfunction sweeping the nation," warns Patricia Hersch, a journalist who spent three years chronicling the lives of eight teenagers.[1]

This unease is compounded in Christian families with the parents' struggle to cope with their children's nearly constant exposure to sex, violence, and consumerism found in our increasingly godless culture. "If one had set out to create a culture purposefully damaging to children," says cultural critic Bill McKibben, "you couldn't do much better than America at the end of the 20th century."[2]

As fears rise and answers seem increasingly elusive, some parents are pointing their fingers at technology; others are blaming the culture industry; still others see the culprit as the government itself. Conscientious fathers and mothers feel powerless. For instance, in a recent *USA Today* poll, 51 percent of parents agreed that "There are so many bad influences out there that even for parents who do a good job, there is a good chance their children will get into serious trouble."[3]

The statistics seem to prove the point. The Carnegie Council on Adolescent Development found that half of all of America's adolescents are at some risk for serious problems: substance abuse, early and unprotected sexual intercourse, dangerous accident-prone lifestyles, delinquent behavior, and dropping out of school. A fourth are at risk for serious multiple high-risk behaviors and school failure.[4]

In this climate, it's easy to see why the how-to parenting books proliferate. And some degree of panic is understandable. But such reactions not only overestimate our role as parents but also undermine our trust in God.

SEE NO EVIL, HEAR NO EVIL

A reaction as equally common as anxiety is denial: We avoid altogether the reality of what our teens are facing. Parental obliviousness can take several forms, such as denial based on fear: "I don't know about my teenager, and I'm afraid to ask." These parents may suspect that their child is into drugs or is having sex, but are too timid to confront the matter directly. In doing so they are—intended or not—abdicating their parental responsibilities.

Another form of denial is based on ignorance, either expressed as "I don't care to know, it's his life," or even more common, "I assume I know what's going on with her." But in reality most parents are ignorant of adolescent culture today; we are largely isolated from the life of our teenager. We don't listen to their music, read their magazines, or spend time in their world. An occasional conversation does not gain us access into our child's life.

This isolation can be seen clearly—and shockingly—in *Being Adolescent*, a study by Mihaly Csikzentmihalyi and Reed Larson. These researchers found that adolescents spend only 4.8 percent of their time with their parents and only 2 percent with adults who are not their parents.[5] This finding has obvious implications for our children, but even greater ramifications for us as parents. For we are generally clueless. Increasingly the period of adolescence has become an "isolated society with its own values, ethics, rules, worldview, rites of passage, worries, joys, and momentum."[6]

"Adolescence" means something fundamentally different to our teenagers than it did in the sixties when we were their age. According to sixteen-year-old Lucy Smith, "Parents think they know what we're going through, because they were our age once, but the world is a different place in 1997 than 1967. Kids in junior high are facing decisions that their parents didn't have to make until college."[7] Behind the visible rituals that we remember lies a very different and troubling world.

Appearances themselves can be deceptive. Parents may be alarmed by kids dressed in the Goth fashion of black clothes, eyeliner, and nail polish; the crimped hair, bracelets, and piercings. Some may be put off by hip-hop and the culture of rap's Gansta chic: baggy pants worn low on the hips; Tommy Hilfiger designer labels blazoned across body parts like a billboard; the teen's distinctive swagger and in-your-face defiance.

But the challenge our children face is not limited to such visible expressions of youthful identity. The same problems and pressures are found even among the "normal" looking young people in our church youth groups. "While adults seem obsessed with controlling what adolescents see, hear, learn, and do, adolescents have to cope day-to-day in a mixed-up world," Hersch warns.[8] Theirs is a world that few Christian parents understand, and even fewer would believe.

Along with the forms of denial based on fear or ignorance is that based on pride or a false sense of parental self-esteem. These are parents who, when confronted with the facts of their child's behavior, rush to deny that their darling could ever do anything wrong: "My Billy never lies." Or, "Cindy may have the pill, but that doesn't mean she's having sex." Or, "Andrew was caught with drugs last semester, but they weren't his; someone put them in his locker."

Parents who avoid facing failure by shielding their children from the consequences of unwise choices provide the most lethal form of denial. Hersch describes the reaction of Courtney and Dee, two teenagers from Reston, Virginia, who were caught with marijuana. Laughing at their parents' naïveté since finding out about their drug use last year, they remarked, "They have got to be either dumb or in denial to believe we would only try drugs once."[9]

BACK TO THE WOMB

The third common reaction of Christian parents is to retreat. Committed mothers and fathers face strong impulses to isolate their children from cultural influences, as seen in the growth of Christian schools and even more so within the homeschooling movement. Dana Mack, a scholar with the Institute for American Values, suggests that parents have begun to rebel against the dominant culture by teaching their own children and giving up an income so that one of the adults can be a full-time parent.[10] Up to 2.5 million children are homeschooled, just over 2 percent of the school-age population.[11]

"The homeschooling family, thinking of maintaining a wholesome and healthy lifestyle for its members, feels obliged not only to withdraw from public education, but also to withdraw from the general popular culture," explains homeschool consultant Samuel Blumenfeld.[12] Debra Bell, author of *The Ultimate Guide to Homeschooling,* agrees: "Crime, drug abuse, and teenage suicide can overwhelm many of us with fear for our kids. Homeschooling is a tactical step to insulate them from these harsher realities."[13]

As a product of homeschooling myself and a strong advocate of educational choice, my point is not to criticize the legitimate educational value of homeschooling. Nor am I questioning the motivation and sacrifices made by homeschooling parents for their children. But we do need to evaluate the assumption that either homeschooling or Christian schooling can isolate our children from the broader cultural influences they will face.

We should ask ourselves the following questions: Is such isolation effective? Or even biblically legitimate? Is it really possible to protect our children from the taken-for-granted assumptions that permeate contemporary life? Does getting rid of our family TV and Internet access alter the overwhelming cultural realities in which our children are being raised? Is it possible to isolate our children, when, for example, they play with other kids at the neighborhood park?

These strategies of isolation and protection become even more dubious when children approach adolescence. Of course parental limits and standards are important. But the notion of being able to raise a child in a sanitized world, untouched by the spirit of our age, is simply naïve—however well-intended and conscientious the parents may be. And is not the world the place to which our children are called to be salt and light as young apprentices of Jesus?

A TEMPORARY STEWARDSHIP

As followers of Christ, we are not to be isolated or insulated from the world. No, we are to be Christ's incarnation in the world working for the extension of His kingdom as we seek to overcome evil with good. Our parenting should reflect these goals.

The aim of Christian parenting is not fundamentally different from the aim of discipleship. Our deepest prayer and desire as parents is that our children will become mature followers of Christ with a clear sense of calling in their life. Parenting is a temporary stewardship in this process.

The time comes when parents must turn their parenting responsibilities over to the Lord. C. S. Lewis writes that the proper aim of the maternal instinct is to work toward its own abdication: "We must aim at making ourselves superfluous. The hour when we can say 'They need me no longer' should be our reward."[14]

One is always a parent, but one does not always parent, as we see in the next chapter.

CHAPTER THREE

From the Heart

CHILDREN NO MORE

When in the development of our children do we begin to let go? For what age do the biblical principles on child-rearing apply? What, in particular, does the Bible say about adolescence? Answering these questions will help us determine how and when to carry out our responsibilities as Christian parents.

Adolescence as a separate youth culture or developmental phase of life is not rooted in the Bible, but is a modern invention. For most of history—and most certainly in the biblical times— adolescents were treated as young adults, not children. Samuel when he received God's call, David when he fought Goliath, and Mary when she became pregnant with Jesus were all likely to be in their teen years.

In medieval society, the idea of childhood itself was virtually unknown. Social historian Philippe Ariés writes in *Centuries of Childhood* that, "It is as if, to every period of history, there corresponds a privileged age and a particular division of human life: 'youth' is the privileged age of the seventeenth century, childhood of the nineteenth, adolescence of the twentieth."[1] In fact, it was only in 1904 that adolescence became a recognized and discrete state of life.[2]

Adolescence emerged from the growing affluence of the Industrial Revolution in the late nineteenth century. Prior to this time, people did not experience an extended transition period where they were without adult responsibilities yet were no longer developmentally children. Instead, they held meaningful jobs and were of economic value to their families. They were either children or adults and were treated as such.

But with the abolition of child labor, the extension of schooling, and the decline in farming, adolescence in this century has become a historically unique social and economic holding period. Some of the tensions associated with adolescence today stem from the artificial boundaries that we place on teenagers; others are rooted in our unwillingness to allow them to experience both the responsibilities and the consequences of their choices.

SEPARATE STANDARDS

Adolescence is the longest it has ever been in recorded history— and getting longer.[3] Social historian Stephanie Coontz writes,

> Relations between adults and teens are especially strained today, not because youths have lost their childhood, as is usually suggested, but because they are not being adequately prepared for the new requirements of adulthood. In some ways, childhood has actually been prolonged, if it is measured by dependence on parents and segregation from adult activities. What many young people have lost are clear paths for gaining experience doing responsible, socially necessary work, either in or out of the home, and for moving away from parental supervision without losing contact with adults.[4]

Take, for example, the American practice of legally restricting alcohol consumption to those who are twenty-one or older. Does such a prohibition really make any moral or sociological sense to an eighteen-year-old adolescent? Those who are eighteen have the right to determine the future leadership of the nation through their vote, can give up their life in service for their country in the draft, can drive twenty-thousand-dollar cars at home and million-dollar vehicles in the military, can sign legal documents, and can enter into a lifelong marriage covenant. Simultaneously, however, they cannot legally drink a beer. Such observations advocate neither underage drinking itself nor irresponsible consumption of alcohol, but merely illustrate the historically recent and legally arbitrary constraints on adolescent behavior.

Up until the last century, few separate standards or different laws distinguished teenagers from adults. What was wrong for teens was wrong for adults. But not so today. Developmentally adults, teenagers are asked to abide by rules and standards no longer held by the vast majority of adults. Coontz observes,

> All premarital sex was supposedly out of line in the nine-teenth century; teen sex was not singled out as a special problem. In fact as late as 1886, the "age of consent" for girls was only 10 in more than half the states in the union. However, girls or women who *did* consent to premarital sex were ostracized, regardless of their age. Today's adults have moved on to new amusements and freedoms, but we want teens to play the old games by the old rules.[5]

The same can be said for so-called "adult" entertainment, which was once seen as no more appropriate for adults than those under the age of seventeen. Teens, it should be noted, are following the example of the adults around them.

LIFE IN THE KINGDOM

If we listen to the voices of teenagers today, we will hear a longing for respect and the desire that adults would acknowledge that their choices matter and their struggles are real. Teens no longer have the physical or emotional dependencies associated with young children. Thus Tedd Tripp acknowledges that "A good metaphor for the parent and teenage child relationship is the relationship adults would have with one another."[6]

Or as C. S. Lewis admonishes,

Who has not been the embarrassed guest at family meals where the father or mother treats their grown-up offspring with an incivility which, offered to any other young people, would simply have terminated the acquaintance? Dogmatic assertions on matters which the children understand and their elders don't, ruthless interruptions, flat contradictions, ridicule of things the young take seriously—sometimes of their religion—insulting references to their friends, all provide an easy answer to the question "Why are they always out? Why do they like every house better than their home?" Who does not prefer civility to barbarism?[7]

At a certain point in our children's development, our role as parents diminishes. By the time they are teenagers, our *authority over* their choices is realistically reduced to having an *influence on* them. The myth of parental control, coupled with a preoccupation with a limited list of behaviors such as smoking, alcohol, sex, and drugs, has encouraged the disparity between what parents observe about their teens' lives and the actual reality that occurs with the adolescents' peers.

Judith Harris observes,

The parents of reasonably well-behaved teenagers don't realize how crucially their ability to monitor their kid's activities depends upon the willing cooperation of the kid. . . . The adolescents who can be monitored are the ones who are willing to be monitored, and they are the ones who need it least. Parents have remarkably little power to maintain control over the adolescents who need it most.[8]

As parents we must remember that anything God wants to achieve in a life will not be accomplished by coercion—His or ours. Life in the kingdom is lived from the heart. For God is not solely interested in words—a child's professions. Nor is He solely interested in behavior—a child's obedience. Rather, God is primarily concerned with the heart—a child's loves as revealed by his or her words and behavior. What God desires is life-long apprentices of Jesus who love Him and love what He loves.

What our children believe influences their decisions, but their choices must always be their own if they are to reflect their hearts' condition. For God has ordained the essence of human personality to be lived from the heart.[9] Dallas Willard writes,

> Children cannot develop into responsible, competent human beings if they are always told what to do. Personality and character are, in their very essence, inner directed. This inner directedness is perfected in redemption. . . . Moreover, children's characters cannot be known, even to themselves, until they are turned loose to do what they want. It is precisely what children want, and how they handle those wants, that both manifests and makes them the people they are.[10]

Christian parenting is not about control and conformity. Children who are compliant and who are no trouble to their parents can be just as far from God as rebellious children who cause parental distress. The older brother was just as estranged from his father as the prodigal son.

BIBLICAL PRINCIPLES OF PARENTING

So, what is Christian parenting? In short, it's loving our children as God loves us. It's emulating the father of the prodigal son who loved him enough to let him leave and squander his inheritance. And it's nothing less than introducing our children to life in the kingdom of God in a developmentally appropriate manner.

Christian parenting assumes that we ourselves are living such a life. For we cannot teach what we do not know; we cannot show what we do not live. We will not reflect the reality of Christ if ours is only a religious facade. Godly parenting is more about who we are as parents than it is about our children. It's more a mirror than a rod.

The biblical principles of parenting must be understood in light of this life in the kingdom. Otherwise, what results are frustrating variations of legalism—in both parent and child. The law is the *course* of rightness, but never the *source*.[11] Christian parenting must influence the source, the will, rather than simply impose the course, the behavior.

The Bible does not tell us everything there is to know about child-rearing, but it does provide basic principles. These guidelines, along with God's goal of life in the kingdom, set the framework for our understanding of parenting. The following are ten key principles from Scripture that set the framework for Christian parenting:

1. Parents are not to place children and family above God.[12]
2. Parents are spiritually responsible to instruct their children in truth and to discipline error.[13]
3. Children are self-determining bearers of the image of God, born sinful and in need of parental discipline.[14]
4. A father's stewardship of his family is a mark of his spiritual maturity.[15]
5. Fathers are not to be unreasonable in their expectations of, or their demands toward, their children.[16]
6. Children are to obey their parents' godly instruction.[17]
7. Children's choices of bad companions will overrule good parental instruction.[18]
8. Children's disobedience of parents is a common characteristic of lawlessness in a society.[19]
9. Children's attitudes toward their godly parents reflect their hearts' attitudes toward authority in general and toward God in particular.
10. Sinful family patterns will influence subsequent generations.[20]

In reviewing these ten biblical principles, we notice immediately that the emphasis is on parents and their responsibilities, and particularly on the father. A qualification for spiritual leadership within the church is based on a father's stewardship of his family life. Although a father cannot finally control whether his children will become believers or will develop rebellious behaviors, a father's failed stewardship of his family can alone disqualify him for spiritual leadership in the larger church community. Such a strict standard is less a sign of parental failure than a reminder of parental priorities.

The Scriptures may not tell us all there is to know about child-rearing, but its principles establish the spiritual importance of our role and set the framework for our loving interaction with our children. To apply the biblical principles meaningfully, we must couple them with an understanding of developmental psychology as well as contemporary youth culture.

To seek to influence teenagers in their choices of the heart, Christian parents must know the world in which their children negotiate day to day. This involves study, observation, and listening. We thus turn in part two to an overview of contemporary youth culture. Understanding the realities facing our teenagers is the first step in wisely exercising our parental responsibilities. Our influence begins with knowledge of their world.

THE CONTEXT OF CHRISTIAN PARENTING

CHAPTER FOUR

The Madman's Warning

"WE'RE SCREWED"

In the summer of 1996, *Rolling Stone* magazine declared that the "Hot Mood" of youth in the nineties was confusion. Will Dana in his article referred to the famous line in W. B. Yeats's poem "The Second Coming": "Things fall apart; the center cannot hold." Writing about contemporary youth culture, Dana said, "We used to think the center couldn't hold. All of a sudden, there doesn't seem to be a center at all."[1] These few words sum up contemporary culture—it's not simply the loss of meaning, but the loss of the *possibility* of meaning.

The repeated refrains of confusion and meaninglessness fill the music of adolescent consciousness. Michael Stipes of the rock group R.E.M. sings, "I can't taste it. I'm tired and naked. I don't know what I'm hungry for. I don't know what I want anymore."[2] Or as Billy Corgan, the lead singer of Smashing Pumpkins, shouts in the song "Zero," "God is empty, just like me."[3]

Are these merely the jaded perspectives of rebellious youths? No, they're the honest reflection of the world bequeathed by generations of adults—a world in which God is functionally dead.

And if God is dead, the blood is largely on our hands. French essayist Montesquieu wrote in his *Spirit of the Laws,* "It is not the young people who degenerate; they are ruined only when grown men have already been corrupted."[4] Likewise Mardi Keyes of L'Abri Fellowship reminds parents, "Resist the temptation to blame the kids. It is the adult generation which has put up such incredible stumbling blocks in the way of young people's growth into maturity."[5] Or as my high-school son said with tears in his eyes after hearing me lecture on postmodern culture, "What you're saying, Dad, is that we're screwed."

Please stay with me as we move into this section—it may be tough going. Moreover, what follows is not found in the typical parenting book. You may be tempted to go straight to the priorities of parenting in section three. But please don't, for the "what" will only make sense if you first understand the "why."

In order to parent wisely, we must examine the depth of the problem we are up against. We will explore the currents and trends of this generation that is growing up without the cultural moorings of Christian faith; unfortunately, the situation is far worse than many Christians think. So for the love of our children, let's learn a little history and philosophy.

THE DEATH OF GOD

A hundred years ago, philosopher Friedrich Nietzsche was anticipating our day when he proclaimed that God is dead. "The story I have to tell," he wrote, "is the history of the next two centuries. . . . Where we live, soon nobody will be able to exist."[6]

Nietzsche in his declaration was not talking about a theological truth but was making a prediction about society. He was being more honest than most Christians in his day or ours in observing that one does not have to be a philosophical atheist to be a practical atheist. For atheists like Nietzsche in both philosophy and practice are rare. What proliferates instead are those who assume that God exists but who live as if that fact doesn't matter much.

German atheistic philosopher Ludwig Feuerbach notes the practical atheism of the modern "believer." This is the person who "denies God practically by his conduct—the world has possession of all his thoughts and inclinations—but he does not deny him theoretically, he does not attack his existence; he lets that rest. But his existence does not affect or incommode him."[7]

Likewise, for Danish philosopher Søren Kierkegaard the opposite of Christianity is not atheism, agnosticism, or any other species of overt secularism, but "Christendom"—secularism pretending to be religious. It is suburban, pasteurized, lukewarm, therapeutic, consumer Christianity "lite."

Nietzsche wandered to the edge of the abyss with his eyes wide open, facing the consequences of the death of God. Much worse, warns philosopher Van Riessen, are those who wander there with their eyes closed, or those who think they can avoid the problem altogether by taking a safer way far from the chasm.[8]

Nietzsche exposes this comfortable practical atheism: "He who no longer finds what is great in God will find it nowhere."[9] He also warns of the enormous cultural consequences resulting from this casual atheism in practice. Indeed, our children are living in its legacy.

DECAYING INTO BANKRUPTCY

Above my desk at the University of Virginia hung a framed quotation of Nietzsche that I kept as a daily reminder of what was at stake in my studies. In seeking to understand and interpret the spirit of our age, I was not blithely pursuing an academic career or chasing a passing intellectual fancy. Instead, I was face to face with a culture of great destructive potential. Its intellectual burden and ensuing cultural battle is spiritual at its core. This is the world facing our children; this is the inevitable context of our parenting.

Let me clarify a key term that I will use throughout this book: "deathwork culture," which is how I interpret the contemporary American scene. The phrase also describes what academics call "postmodern culture." Many scholars, mostly philosophers and theologians in my experience, and including many Christians, view postmodernism in a positive light. I do not.

Of course, I'm aware of the intellectual contributions of postmodernism: its openness to alternative views, its critique of rationalism, and its appreciation for community, to name a few. But to resort to a metaphor, postmodernism goes too far in its critique of modernism, throwing the baby out with the bath water. In addition, the danger is not simply how postmodernity plays out in theory, but how it works out in real life.

By the end of this analysis, you will be able to decide for yourself if "deathwork" is too negative a term. I fear not. But then, I digress. Back to my desk in the basement of Garrett Hall at the University of Virginia.

The quotation that hung before my eyes is from a story Nietzsche told of a madman who rushes into the marketplace with an urgent warning that no one heeds. He laments, "People have no notion yet that from now onwards they exist on the mere pittance of inherited and decaying values—soon to be overtaken by an enormous bankruptcy."[10] Disheartened, the madman leaves, knowing that his words will be later fulfilled. Here is his warning, which applies now:

> "Where has God gone? I shall tell you. We have killed him—you and I. *We are all his murderers.* But how have we done this? How were we able to drink up the sea? Who gave us the sponge to wipe away the entire horizon? What did we do when we unchained this earth from the sun . . . ? Do we not hear anything yet of the noise of the gravediggers who are burying God? *Do we not smell anything yet of God's decomposition?*—gods, too, decompose. God is dead. God remains dead. And we have killed him. How shall we, the murderers of all murderers, console ourselves? That which was holiest and mightiest of all that the world has yet possessed has bled to death under our knives—who will wipe this blood off us? With what water could we purify ourselves? *What festivals of atonement, what sacred games shall we need to invent?* Is not the greatness of this deed too great for us? Must we not ourselves become gods simply to seem worthy of it? There has never been a greater deed. . . ."

Here the madman fell silent and again regarded his listeners; and they, too, were silent and stared at him in astonishment. At last he threw his lantern to the ground and it broke and went out. "I come too early," he said then;

"my time has not yet come. This tremendous event is still on its way, still traveling—it has not yet reached the ears of men. Lightning and thunder require time, deeds require time after they have been done before they can be seen and heard. This deed is still more distant from them than the most distant stars—*and yet they have done it themselves.*"[11]

Nietzsche in the late 1800s was pointing to our present deathwork culture. In this chapter, I will give a brief historical overview explaining how contemporary society has come to this woeful place. In chapter five, I will explore the stealth factor—the role of culture itself—before moving in chapters six and seven to suggest the basic contours of our deathwork culture. Then in chapter eight, I will show how this deathwork dominates youth culture, and in chapter nine, why it matters.

It may seem like hard work, but as parents we must come to terms with these cultural realities because of the seriousness of the task before us. Prescribing aspirin is not an effective treatment for cancer. Nor is sending Cub Scouts to fight a forest fire. Nor is casually turning over our adolescent children to a youth pastor. As parents, we must wake up and face what is at stake in our children's world. For although the cultural realities rooted in Nietzsche's proclamation affect us all, they are compounded and amplified in youth culture. Let us turn first to an examination of how we got here.

ADVANCING HUMANITY

Every civilization and period of history has a unifying story that defines its aspirations. The medieval story was one of *providence*—history was seen as the unfolding of God's guiding hand. The Enlightenment story, in turn, was based on *progress*—the expanding reach of reason. And the contemporary story is based on *preference*—the consumer choice of whatever story one wants. Another way of looking at the rise of the contemporary consciousness is the shift in authority from God to Nature to Self. This progression is the substance of what high-school students are taught in their European history course.

To explain further, the initial move from God to reason came about from the Renaissance artists and humanists who valued individual achievement and an increasingly earthly orientation to life. This led to the Scientific Revolution in the seventeenth century, which provided a new method of inquiry and demonstrated the power and self-sufficiency of the human intellect. Through reason alone, they believed, the general principles that operate both the physical and social world could be uncovered. Divine revelation was no longer needed, and its relevance was reduced to an increasingly confined sphere of life.

The application of scientific reason alone to an analysis of nature, government, religion, law, economics, and education came to be known as the Enlightenment Project. In making no reference to the claims of revelation, it was essentially secular. Intellectual historian Richard Tarnas writes,

> [It] reflected a gradual but finally radical shift of psychological allegiance from God to man, from dependence to independence, from otherworldliness to this world, from transcendent to empirical, from faith to fact, from universals to particulars, from a supernaturally created cosmos to a naturally evolving cosmos, from a fallen humanity to an advancing one. . . . Science gave man a new faith—not only in knowledge, but in himself.[12]

The two centuries in which confidence in this secular vision held sway are represented by the symbolic bookends of 1789 and 1989—from the *philosophes* and the French Revolution to the collapse of communism and fall of the Berlin Wall.

The high watermark of the Enlightenment Project is perhaps seen best in the imperialist attitudes of the late nineteenth century. Rudyard Kipling expressed the prevailing sentiments of his day in his poem, "The White Man's Burden" (1899). In it he calls on England to send the "best ye breed" to bring the benefits of the West to "your new-caught, sullen peoples, half devil and half child."[13] The moral burden and glory of the Western white man lay in civilizing the pagan savages of the East. Kipling was unflinchingly confident in the superiority of the West.

But seventeenth-century mathematician and Christian apologist Blaise Pascal knew at the outset that the Enlightenment was off to a bad start. "I cannot forgive Descartes," he wrote of his contemporary in his *Pensées*.[14] As the philosophical father of the Enlightenment Project, Descartes gave initial lip service to God but then dispensed with Him in relying on reason alone.

Pascal foresaw the inevitable consequences and imagined what God would say to the Enlightenment philosophers of his day: "You wanted to make yourself your own center and do without my help. You withdrew from my rule, setting yourself up as my equal in your desire to find happiness in yourself, and I abandoned you to yourself."[15] Man abandoned to man is man left to his own devices, and the results are predictable. The death of God leads to the death of man. As C. S. Lewis observes, "Man's final conquest has proved to be the abolition of man."[16]

BLOOD ON OUR HANDS

We have witnessed firsthand the results of man abandoned to himself as we close the bloodiest century in world history. Our unquestioned confidence in the Enlightenment Project has now been muted or largely abandoned. Historian A.J.P. Taylor summarizes the feeling of many of his generation:

> The First World War was difficult to fit into the picture of a rational civilization advancing by ordered stages. The civilized men of the twentieth century had outdone in savagery the barbarians of all preceding ages, and their civilized virtues — organization, mechanical skill, self-sacrifice — had made war's savagery all the more terrible. Modern man had developed powers, which he was not fit to use. European civilization had been weighed in the balance and found wanting.[17]

Of course, we can add to Taylor's observation Hitler's Holocaust, Stalin's purges, Mao's Cultural Revolution, Pol Pot's genocide, and Milosevic's ethnic cleansing.

Progress in our century, it appears, comes at a terrible price.

For instance, the total number of twentieth-century battle deaths are approximately 36 million. And the number of deaths related to twentieth-century totalitarianism are close to 95 million.

Consequently, the contemporary intellectual world has largely abandoned the confidence in reason that fueled the Enlightenment. Moreover, our century's atrocities have made thinkers suspicious of any claim of universal knowledge or absolute truth—whether Christian or scientific. Any overarching story that gives a comprehensive meaning to life is greeted with skepticism. There is no grand narrative that explains life, only personal plots.

Without God as a transcendent mooring, modern man has found that autonomous reason leaves him alone and adrift. In the words of theologian John Dominic Crossan: "There is no light-house keeper. There is no lighthouse. There is no dry land. There are only people living on rafts made from their own imaginations."[18]

This is the dominant perspective taught in the classes of our nation's universities. For example, take Richard Rorty, one of the nation's most influential postmodern philosophers who taught to standing-room-only classes at the University of Virginia. He summarizes his beliefs in this way:

> [O]nce upon a time we felt a need to worship something, which lay beyond the visible world. Beginning in the seventeenth century, we tried to substitute a love of truth for a love of God, treating the world described by science as a quasi divinity. Beginning at the end of the eighteenth century we tried to substitute a love of ourselves for a love of scientific truth, a worship of our own deep spiritual or poetic nature, treated as one more quasi divinity . . . [and now we have arrived at] the point where we no longer worship anything, where we treat nothing as a quasi divinity, where we treat everything—our language, our conscience, our community—as a product of time and chance.[19]

Such views are hardly limited to the academic elite. Listen to sixteen-year-old Kristin Johnson: "One concept that really fascinates me is post-modern thinking—the idea that there is no absolute truth, and how all history is relative. . . . We rewrite it according to how we want to see it and how we are able to see it, given our own time and place in history."[20] Ours would seem to be a world where life's foundations are rooted in time plus chance plus the impersonal. In such a world, Nietzsche is right: God is dead.

Charles Darwin, an influential contemporary of Nietzsche, noted, "A man who has no assured and ever-present belief in the existence of a personal God or of a future existence with retribution or reward, can have for his rule of life, as far as I can see, only to follow those impulses which are strongest or which seem to him the best ones."[21] Exactly. And such is the world portrayed daily in our culture through television, film, and song.

High-school teachers live in fear of teenage violence. College administrators wrestle to curb binge drinking. Yet why are we so surprised by these behaviors? Both are only the manifestations of a culture-wide system of belief—a belief in power and pleasure— that pervades youth culture and is celebrated by it.

President Clinton won an election with the phrase "It's the economy, stupid!" As parents we need to wake up to the fact that "It's the culture, stupid!" It is to this stealth factor that we now turn.

CHAPTER FIVE

The Stealth Factor

GUITARS, GUNS, AND GOODNESS

In an article in *Rolling Stone,* its editor, Jann Wenner, bemoaned William Bennett's "moral grandstanding" against rock music. "Music is not the catalyst for violence," Wenner explains. "The lyrics of rappers and heavy-metal bands certainly have no more effect on children than the graphic staple-gun scenes in the PG-rated, ostensibly family oriented *Home Alone* movies."[1]

Wenner protests too much. It does matter what attitudes are depicted in the riffs and raps pulsing from one's Walkman because ideas have consequences. And pop icons serve to inspire the moral imagination of their fans.

Wenner suggests that if Bennett truly wants to clean up popular culture, he should focus on eradicating guns, as surely guitars never killed anyone. I suspect that Wenner understands the power of music in the lives of adolescents but doesn't want to admit it when criticized. For guitars are not the challenge to goodness, but the lyrics and lifestyles of those who wield them are.

Or listen to Marilyn Manson (also known as Brian Warner), who was awarded the best new artist in the 1997 *Rolling Stone* reader's poll.[2] A shock rocker similar to Trent Reznor of Nine Inch Nails, he recently responded in *Rolling Stone* to the charges that his music was behind the atrocity at Columbine High School: "It is sad to think that the first few people on earth needed no books, movies, games or music to inspire cold-blooded murder. The day that Cain bashed his brother Abel's brains in, the only motivation he needed was his own human disposition to violence."[3] This half-truth is a bit disingenuous from an artist who sells T-shirts at his concerts with "KILL YOUR PARENTS" emblazoned on the fronts.

Scottish patriot Andrew Fletcher wrote in 1704 what the rockers are not saying out loud: "If a man were permitted to make all the ballads, he need not care who should make the laws of a nation." What Fletcher is underlining is the often-unheeded stealth factor—the importance of culture. By this I mean the taken-for-granted way we understand ourselves, others, and the larger world, and the way we order our experience.

As Christians and parents we have not taken culture seriously enough, and this in a day of a deathwork culture spawned by a practical atheism that takes no prisoners. The stakes are high; the solutions are demanding; the challenges to parenting are immense. Thus we must understand first what culture itself is, and then learn about the contours of the deathwork culture in which our teenagers spend their days and their nights.

UNNOTICED AND UNHEEDED

Culture is inherently invisible. It's what seems natural and normal and thus needs no explanation. Sociologist Alfred Schutz describes it as the "natural attitude": "I always find myself in a world which is for me taken for granted and self-evidently 'real.' I was born into it and I assume that it existed before me. It is the unexamined ground of everything in my experience, as it were, the taken-for-granted frame in which all the problems which I must overcome are placed."[4]

Dallas Willard, in turn, describes culture as "an anonymous and many-faceted structure of 'authority' that stipulates what is to count as knowledge and reality."[5] C. S. Lewis adds that "It is not the books written in direct defense of Materialism that make modern man a materialist; it is the materialistic assumptions in all the other books."[6] Thus it's not primarily sex-education books that undermine teenage chastity, but the casual assumption of fornication in Nicholas Sparks' *Message in a Bottle* (1999) and "therapeutic" adultery in Robert Waller's *The Bridges of Madison County* (1995).

Our lives are shaped by this surrounding world more than by the works of renowned thinkers. The great devotional writer A. W. Tozer was fond of saying that people "are influenced more by their common, everyday thinking than by any rare intellectual feat such as writing a great poem or painting a famous picture. Feats of thinking may create a reputation, but habits of thinking create character."[7] Culture shapes our habits. Habits shape our character. Character shapes our destiny.

This taken-for-granted culture is also what the Bible calls the visible world or *kosmos*. When we pray the Lord's Prayer, "your kingdom come, your will be done on earth" (Matthew 6:10), we're talking about culture. When we are commanded to "not conform any longer to the pattern of this world" (Romans 12:2), Paul's writing about culture.

THE SUBTLE AND SEDUCTIVE WHISPER

But culture is not all bad. In fact, it is the arena in which we are to express God's intention for human existence at creation. The gospel mandate is a summons to life in the kingdom, an invitation for us to be coworkers in advancing the sphere where Jesus' authority and rule acknowledged and made reality. As J. Gresham Machen described the cultural task,

> Christianity must pervade not merely all nations, but also all human thought. The Christian, therefore, cannot be indifferent to any branch of earnest human endeavor. . . . It must be studied either in order to be demonstrated as false, or else in order to be made useful in advancing the Kingdom of God. . . . The Church must seek to conquer not merely every man for Christ, but also the whole of man.[8]

But culture is also contested terrain. Because it is where sin is institutionalized, it can be coercive to our thoughts and behaviors.

One of the great challenges of discipleship is to become aware of the world's sinful patterns so that we can learn to resist them through Christ's power, thereby bringing them into conformity to Christ.

This is why the deathwork culture sneaks up on us—life seems to be going along as "normal" and we explain away the bad things that sometimes happen as the work of some deranged individual or some isolated event. Yet we are more a part of this craziness than we would ever care to realize. Such is the power of culture—it largely defines for us what is thinkable and what is real.

For most of us, cultural change takes place without our noticing. That is the way culture works—incrementally, invisibly, and irresistibly. Culture does not shout, it whispers. "Control the layout, the atmosphere, the background music, those shapings that shape us constantly and yet mindlessly just beneath the level of our attention, and we will move where you want us to and reliably 'choose' what you have preselected," observes sociologist David Bosworth.[9]

In addition, we should note that cultural changes are the delayed consequences of ideas held a generation ago. Each generation is taught by the one earlier. C. S. Lewis observes, "We talk of the views of contemporary adolescence as if some peculiarity in contemporary adolescence had produced them out of itself. In reality, they are usually a delayed result—for the mental world also has its time-bombs—of obsolete adolescence, now middle-aged and dominating its form room."[10] Teens today are the true children of the sixties.

THE DEATHWORK LOGIC

My point in all of this is simply to underline that the deathwork culture—the world where God is dead—is inescapable. Its values are entrenched within the academia, entertainment, the media, and the government—institutions that are uniquely "culture forming." In short, the deathwork culture is like the air around us; it is everywhere and is as unconscious as the last breath we drew as we read this sentence.

The deathwork culture has a clear logic. The assumption of autonomy is followed by unfettered passions, which leads to belief in a world without limits. Put simply, pride and lust end in license. Hundreds of years ago, Blaise Pascal anticipated the cultural consequences of this process.

> Your chief maladies are pride that takes you from God, and lust, which binds you to earth; and they have done nothing else but cherish one or the other of these diseases. If they gave you God as an end, it was only to administer to your pride; they made you think that you are by nature like Him, and conformed to Him. And those who saw the absurdity of this claim put you on the other precipice, by making you understand that your nature was like that of the brutes, and led you to seek your good in the lusts which are shared by the animals.[11]

The deathwork culture is the logical consequence of this process. Nietzsche himself warned of our day: "I foresee something terrible, Chaos everywhere. Nothing left which is of any value; nothing which commands: Thou shalt!"[12]

RAISED WITHOUT GOD

Sadly, this is the world our children have inherited. This is the "first generation raised without religion," writes Douglas Coupland, who first coined the term "Generation X" as a loose description of those following the Baby Boomers. "What happens if we are raised without religion or beliefs? . . . We are all living creatures with strong religious impulses, yet where do these impulses flow in a world of malls and TV, Kraft dinners and jets?"[13]

We do not have to look far to see the answer to this question. The thrill of sex and violence, the mind-numbing diversion of drugs and alcohol, the high of mosh pits and rave concerts are all around us. Take, for instance, Marilyn Manson, who *Rolling Stone* describes as "a pop icon who encourages people to question the existence of God and believe in themselves."[14]

Or as Manson himself explains on his Web page,

There are two things that Marilyn Manson has been designed to do. It's been designed to speak to people who understand it and to scare the people who don't. A lot of what I say to our fans is, "Stop worrying about trying to fit into the status quo of what is beautiful and politically correct. Believe in yourself and stick to what's right. If you wanna be like me, then be like yourself." It's the whole Nietzsche philosophy of you are your own God.[15]

In this deathwork culture of "you are your own God," adults anxiously wonder why kids are killing kids in Jonesboro, Paducah, and Littleton. Other parents flinch at the news of a high-school senior giving birth in a hotel bathroom and then throwing the baby in the trash in order to return to the prom dance floor. But in such a deathwork culture, who's surprised?

And in such a culture, who's to blame? Not the kids, as Michael Josephson writes in *Ethical Values, Attitudes, and Behaviors in American Schools:* "The ethics of this generation are but an 'amplified echo' of the worst moral message of their elders. They have grown up in the quicksand of an ambivalent moral society."[16]

In 1924, a year before the famous Scopes trial, Clarence Darrow found himself defending Nathan Leopold and Richard Loeb, two college students who murdered a boy for the intellectual experience. "Is there any blame attached because somebody took Nietzsche's philosophy seriously and fashioned his life on it?" Darrow reasoned. "Your Honor, it is hardly fair to hang a nineteen-year-old boy for the philosophy that was taught him at the university."[17]

I have described contemporary culture, and particularly that of our youth, as a deathwork. We have looked briefly at its sources and have seen that it is inescapable. We now examine its contours — the way it plays out in our daily lives.

Hubris and Hedonism

THE SELF RULES

The first premise of the deathwork culture is the *unquestioned authority of the self*. Nothing trumps the self—not revelation, tradition, reason, or politics. "Where older moral orders looked to a transcendent being, to a covenantal community, to natural law, or to divine reason to provide the substantive basis for culture's moral boundaries, the therapeutic ethos establishes the self as the ultimate object of allegiance," writes Williams College sociologist James Nolan. "Where once the self was to be surrendered, denied, sacrificed, and died to, now the self is to be esteemed, actualized, affirmed and unfettered."[1]

The shift in the location of authority is from that which is outside the self to that which is inside. What is outside constrained the self, but what is within liberates it. This Copernican Revolution of authority has been reinforced principally by two powerful social institutions: psychology and business.[2] Psychology provides the rationale and business the delivery system of the new worldview.

Psychology is the "unreligion of the age, and its master science," writes Philip Rieff in his seminal work, *The Triumph of the Therapeutic*.[3] Therapists are the new secular priests, intoning advice on TV talkshows and supermarket checkout stands. Their couches have replaced church pews as the search for salvation is supplanted by the state of one's emotional health. "What [John] Bradshaw offers is 'lite' religion," explains cultural critic James Twitchell, "free of a vengeful God, free of parental taboos, free of mystery, and, with the exception of daily communion with the inner child, free of demands."[4]

Hollywood glamorizes the priority and authority of the self so that it colors everything, making it difficult to see reality in any other way. Actress Gina Gershon, star of the film *Showgirls* (1995) and ABC's television drama *Snoops* (1999), expresses her preoccupation with self in *Interview* magazine: "Life's about being comfortable with yourself, and that's what I try to be. It sounds simple, but it can be hard. I believe in knowing your own truth, but everyone's truth is different. Where I draw my lines is going to be different from where you draw your lines. It's like Jesus said: 'Know thyself'—the two smartest words ever spoken."[5] Not only are these not Jesus' words, but He actually said something quite different: "Give up your self, and you will find your real self."

At its heart, the deathwork culture is the opposite of the kingdom of God. If God is dead and the self rules, then this is exactly what we would expect to find—the kingdom of man *posing* as the kingdom of God.

COME TO THE CARNIVAL

Moreover, business, once the champion of tradition, is now the instrument of its destruction.[6] Self-fulfillment and rebellion are dominant themes in youth-oriented advertising. Tommy Hilfiger, for instance, began advertisements in 1998 portraying "come-hither" blondes lounging on the President's desk and squatting on the Oval Office rug. And Abercrombie & Fitch's 1998 "Back to School" catalog offers "Drinking 101," a recipe guide for shooters with such names as "Brain Hemorrhage," "Dirty Girl Scout Cookie," "Come in with Me," "Foreplay," "Orgasm," and "Sex on the Beach." Conveniently included is a wall-spinner for drinking games. Cultural critic Tom Frank writes,

Corporate America is not an oppressor but a sponsor of
fun, provider of lifestyle accouterments, facilitator of carnival, our slang-speaking partner in the quest for that
ever-more apocalyptic orgasm. The countercultural idea
has become the capitalist orthodoxy, . . . its taste for self-
fulfillment and its intolerance for the confines of tradition
now permitting vast latitude in consuming practices and
lifestyle experimentation. . . . Advertising teaches us not
in the ways of puritanical self-denial, but in orgiastic
never-ending self-fulfillment."[7]

"Between them," sociologist Robert Bellah concludes, "the
therapist and the manager largely define the outlines of twentieth-
century American culture."[8] The deathwork culture is the merger
in extreme of these two American themes—*freedom* of the self for
the *choice* of desire. Individual freedom and consumer choice are
taken to lengths never before seen or anticipated.

DESIGNER SPIRITUALITY

Nowhere is this illustrated more clearly than in contemporary
forms of pop spirituality. Spirituality is hip today—the January
1999 issue of *Spin*, a progressive youth culture magazine, cites it
as a "big-ass trend." Indeed, growing numbers of Baby Boomers
are being attracted by secular spirituality as they negotiate
midlife and reflect on the vanity of the pursuits that have dominated their lives.[9]

Modern spirituality is a noninstitutional, individualist, subjective, syncretistic, do-it-yourself religion. Take, for instance, the
cover of the July-August 1998 issue of *Utne Reader:* "Designer
God: In a mix-and-match world, why not create your own religion?" Spirituality today is largely a divine deli where consumers
pick and choose among increasingly exotic pagan alternatives.[10]
Traditional boundaries between religions are dissolving as people
tend toward a personalized mix of religious beliefs where they are
at home in many different faiths without claiming a complete allegiance to any.

Tom Beaudoin argues in *Virtual Faith* that "Instead of investing their hearts in doctrine or an institution, people are working out their spirituality through popular culture."[11] Richard Cimino and Don Lattin found the same trend in *Shopping for Faith: American Religion in the New Millennium*. "As the entertainment media becomes the primary conveyor of common culture, it will compete with religious groups as the main bearer of spiritual and religious insight, no matter how mundane and homogenized those revelations may be."[12]

Pop spirituality is largely a return to variants of pantheism, the belief that divinity is inseparable from and immanent in nature. Art historian Camille Paglia argues that "Popular culture is an eruption of paganism. . . . Judeo-Christianity never defeated paganism but rather drove it underground, from which it constantly erupts in all kinds of ways."[13] Neopagan themes dominate contemporary film as well, from Robin Williams' *What Dreams May Come* (1999) to Steven Lucas's *Star Wars Episode I: The Phantom Menace* (1999).[14] Such is the appeal of astrology, crystals, and feng shui. The next big thing will be homes with pagan altars, says Wendy Sarasohn of the Corcoran Group real estate company.[15]

The pagan influence can also be seen in popular magazines. Pamela Fiori, editor-in-chief of *Town & Country*, kicks off her 1999 issue with their first twelve-month guide to astrology. She explains, "*Town & Country* has published a monthly Horoscopes column for decades. It has, by now, become an institution not to be tampered with. Even solid citizens who scoff at Santa Claus and the tooth fairy tell me that they faithfully follow the predictions of our astrologer."[16] C. S. Lewis wryly observes, "Children are not deceived by fairy-tales; they are often and gravely deceived by school-stories. Adults are not deceived by science-fiction; they can be deceived by the stories in women's magazines."[17]

When we examine theoretical pantheism more closely, we see that it quickly degenerates into practical "me-theism." The worship of nature soon becomes the worship of one's own nature—even the spiritualizing of one's instincts, bordering on autoeroticism. Neale Donald Walsch's series *Conversations with God* is a multiyear, runaway best seller in which his central argument is simply that God is me:

Blessed are the Self-centered, for they shall know God. . . .
The highest good is that which produces the highest good
for you. . . . A thing is only right or wrong because you say
it is. A thing is not right or wrong intrinsically. . . . So be
ready, kind soul. For you will be vilified and spat upon . . .
from the moment you accept and adopt your holy cause —
the realization of Self.[18]

Ruth Shalit adds that the new interest in angels is a "civic religion of self-regard." The authors of *Angel Answers* assure us, "The
angels haven't come into our lives so that we can bask in their
divine light. They have come to help us see our own luminous
beauty." Or as the authors of *The Angelspeak Book of Prayer and
Healing* counsel, "It is time to focus on you. Time to tell the angels
what you would like to be, to do, or to have."[19] An insight from
Catholic apologist G. K. Chesterton proves timely here: "That
Jones shall worship the god within him turns out ultimately to
mean that Jones shall worship Jones."[20]

SELF, SEX, AND SPIRITUALITY

Paganism is spirituality attuned to the spirit of the age, for in the
end it celebrates self and sex. *Spin's* Erik Davis observes, "Mystical
options such as yoga and pop cabala offer direct access to deeper
essence, without the pesky moral codes of conventional religion.
Unfortunately, this search can easily degenerate into another
American cult of the self."[21] Pop spirituality takes the same predictable course pantheism has from the beginning of time: A
personal deity offers a personal morality reinforced by a personal
power, which ends in the worship of the person and his or her
passions. "They exchanged the truth of God for a lie, and wor-
shiped and served created things rather than the Creator"
(Romans 1:25).

Paganism always ends in the violent and orgiastic. Chesterton
again observes, "A man loves Nature in the morning for her innocence and amiability, and at nightfall, if he is loving her still, it is
for her darkness and her cruelty."[22] Paganism is a theology of
hubris and hedonism.

Pop spirituality, then, becomes the highest form of self-worship—the divination of ego, the spiritualizing of desire.[23] This is a religion of therapeutic consumerism: cosmic meaning without personal morality; self-affirmation without self-constraint. Jewel, whose 1994 debut album *Pieces of You* sold over 10 million copies, asks, "Who will save your soul, if you won't save your own?"[24]

Who's my savior? Who's in charge? I am. Chesterton warns, "Of all horrible religions the most horrible is the worship of the god within."[25] Film critic David Denby adds, "Culturally, America can only be called neopagan, a hedonistic visual-aural carnival, devoted to popular music, the good life, and the ideals of beauty, and sensual health. Fashion, movies, MTV, the local gym—the blond beasts are us."[26] Nietzsche's Superman is more than a cartoon character. He is the everyman of the deathwork culture.

If the self is the god in charge, then the self must also be creator. Astute Christians will immediately sense the inversion of truth warned of in Romans 1: The normal is seen as deviant and the deviant normal. Amorality becomes accepted as morality. Reality itself becomes indistinguishable from illusion.

Such is the character of the deathwork. Our culture is working out this process of inversion to its logical extreme—a world without boundaries. It's hard to believe we have come this far.

CHAPTER SEVEN

World Without Boundaries

THE LOGIC OF LICENSE

If the logic of the deathwork culture is self-affirmation without self-constraint, then it only takes a small step to suggest that objective reality is also a self-projection. The logical consequence of the deathwork culture is that *reality, or at least our perceptions and understanding of it, is entirety self-made.* More and more people in everyday life are beginning to follow the lead of the deathwork vanguard, which advocates that truth is made rather than found.[1]

Some champions of the deathwork, who are more politically or sociologically oriented, may emphasize the social construction of reality—that reality is the collective decision of a group. Others, who are more psychologically or commercially oriented, emphasize the individual construction of one's personal reality—that reality is little other than the externalization of ego or merely a consumer choice. But in either understanding, central is the belief that nothing exists except what we decide to put there. Ultimate objective reality evaporates, leaving only useful fictions or subjective whims.[2] "Reality," "truth," and "identity" have each become a consumer choice.

ILLUSION OF REALITY

Thirty years ago historian Daniel Boorstin expressed concern over the artifice of an "image-saturated" culture. "We are the first people to live within our illusions," he warned.[3] Or as Jean Baudrillard writes, "Illusion is no longer possible, because the real is no longer possible."[4] All reality is virtual reality. Mark Taylor, professor of humanities at Williams College, adds, "As reality is virtualized, we gradually are forced to confess that real has always been imaginary."[5]

The deathwork culture is a world of surfaces and profound superficiality. A number of years ago, my youngest son and I were visiting Universal Studios in Orlando, Florida. As we looked at the facades of movie sets, the tour guide remarked, "In Orlando, only what you see is real." Reality is an illusion and Hollywood, the grand illusion-maker, is now America's cultural center.

If reality is merely a fiction, then the best fiction is that which is most real. A good fake is to be preferred over a poor reality. Architecture critic Ada Louise Huxtable laments this turn: "What concerns me as much as the state of American building is the American state of mind, in which illusion is preferred over reality to the point where the replica is accepted as genuine. . . . Surrogate experiences and surrogate environments have become the American way of life."[6]

Huxtable tells of the time when moviemakers planned a film about the Alamo. They found the Texas landmark small and unimposing, so they built a bigger and better one in a nearby town. Today both the false and the real are equally popular tourist attractions. Such is the logic of the deathwork: the totalitarianism of ideology has been replaced by the nihilism of illusion.

We are getting to the place where we cannot tell the real from the fake or the illusion from reality. More importantly, we don't even care to make the distinction. Herein lies the danger, for replacing the real with an illusion is the essence of sin. Leanne Payne writes, "Sin has to do, in a very real sense, with rebelliously demanding to experience what is not—what God did not create and can never look upon, much less bless."[7]

SELF-INTEREST OF TRUTH

If "reality" is really an illusion, so too is "truth" only a useful fiction. To quote Nietzsche, truth is "the sum of human relations, which have been enhanced, transposed, and embellished poetically and rhetorically and which after long use seem firm, canonical, and obligatory to people."[8] He is claiming that truth is made up of the fictions that over time become accepted as nonfictions.

Likewise morality, Nietzsche argues, is also based on a process of self-deception. Religion and morality are self-creations that have been sold to us as being absolutely true or objectively real for reasons that hide self-interest. Because everyone's self-interest is different, reality and morality are always plural. There is no one right answer, but only a diversity of competing answers based on competing interests.[9] For if reality is a social construction and truth a useful fiction, then the legitimacy of any viewpoint is found in the solidarity it provides with those who perceive life in the same way. *Waking Ned Divine* (1999) is a cinematic exposition of this view of communal truth.[10]

Richard Rorty argues that "we should think of our sense of community as having no foundation except shared hope and the truth created by such sharing."[11] His emphasis on community rather than individuals gives his type of relativistic pragmatism its political force. Yet as individuals choose to associate with this or that group and this or that compelling fiction, the authority of consumer choice remains with the individual. As philosopher Richard Bernstein observes, "For Rorty there never seem to be any effective constraints on *me* and *my* interpretations. This is why Rorty's constant references to 'we,' a common tradition, a shared consensus appear to be hollow—little more than a label for a projected 'me.'"[12] Tribalism is only me-theism in political dress.

The Eleventh Commandment in such a culture is "Thou shalt not judge," as sociologist Alan Wolfe found when he examined the moral outlook of the suburban middle class. The "reluctance to exclude turns out to be as powerful, if not more powerful, a moral force as a requirement to believe."[13] If all truths are equally true, then all are equally false and no single one has to be taken more seriously than another.

People find themselves more tolerant of others' beliefs, but less certain of their own. "The freedom of our day," declares a Harvard valedictorian, "is the freedom to devote ourselves to any values we please, on the mere condition that we do not believe them to be true."[14]

This type of thinking obviously fragments social groups rather than unifies them, turning contemporary society tribal. Every group hangs on to its chosen fictions and then competes for turf. As the once-benign fictions that promoted the interests of a particular tribe become institutionalized, they become weapons of power. Knowledge becomes power, namely the power to control the spin. "Truth," in turn, is spin that has been accepted and reinforced by the spindoctors in power. In a world of interest-driven fictions, those who pay the piper pick the tune.

Those who believe their viewpoints have been eclipsed, in turn, are angry. Consider the views of rock group Rage Against The Machine, whose 1992 release was called "one of the best hard-rock records ever made" by James Rotondi of Amazon.com. The cover shows a Buddhist monk in the process of self-emulation. In the song, "Take the Power Back," lead singer/writer Zack de la Rocha cries out:

So-called facts are fraud
They want us to allege and pledge
And bow down to their God
Lost the culture, the culture lost
Spun our minds and through time
Ignorance has taken over
We gotta take the power back
Bam, here's the plan
Mother f—Uncle Sam
Step back, I know who I am
Raise up your ear, I'll drop the style and clear
It's the beats and lyrics they fear
The rage is relentless
We need a movement with a quickness
You are the witness to change

And to counteract
We gotta take the power back.[15]

Clearly, one does not have to read Nietzsche or Rorty to capture the spirit of the deathwork culture. Just sit back and turn on the Walkman or the TV.

In all of this, what's true? Whatever I say is true and I have the power to enforce. But as Catholic philosopher Michael Novak rightly observes, "To surrender the claims of truth upon humans is to surrender Earth to thugs."[16] Without truth, facts, or objectivity, all that remains is will and power—a war of all against all.

MASK OF IDENTITY

If nothing out there is a "given," then certainly nothing about an individual is a given either. The self is made, not found. We are the masks we create and wear. The individual in search of self-identity becomes the consummate consumer of reality, from gender to lifestyle. The branding of self consists of attitude, fashion, and lifestyle—namely one's "style." If Martha Stewart is the symbol of the stable identity, then Madonna is the symbol of its variability, from material girl to maternal spirituality.

Business megaconsultant Tom Peters continues in this vein: "Regardless of age, regardless of position, regardless of the business we happen to be in, all of us need to understand the importance of branding. We are CEOs of our own companies: Me, Inc. To be in business today, our most important job is to be head marketer for the brand called YOU."[17] The mother of all self-promotional tools is the on-line branding of a personal Web page. "According to Web wizard Nathan Shearoff, creating your personal Web site is less a technical challenge than an emotional one. Once you've answered the question 'What is your brand?' you're ready to create the brand called URL."[18]

We can see this consumer orientation toward identity formation in the teenage billboards who advertise the latest designer label or rock group on their bodies; in the proliferation of cosmetic surgery, tattoos, and body piercings; in the rise of gender politics; in the popularity of virtual chat rooms and cybersex; in the megastatus afforded fashion models; in the necessity of impression management by business and political leaders; in the ubiquitous therapeutic talkshow experts on daytime TV.

Sexuality, personhood, and the body have each been transformed by the emerging conceptions of the self. How else do we explain the assumptions behind the tequila advertisement that runs in many youth-oriented publications? The two-page spread features an attractive woman in the distance, clad in a bikini. "She's brunette, beautiful and walking toward you," the ad copy reads on its first page. Turn the page over and we see the same picture but the following words: "She's a he. Life's harsh; your tequila shouldn't be." Today one's personhood is not as certain as one's liquor.

Or as the cover of the September-October 1998 issue of *Utne Reader* asks, "It's 2 A.M. Do you know what sex you are? Does anybody?" Nothing is fixed anymore, even the core of one's being. Thus we're not surprised when country-and-western megastar Garth Brooks adopts the elaborate new identity of an Australian alternative rock-star for his album *The Life of Chris Gaines* (1999), complete with biography for his alter ego. Multiple personality disorder opens the door to multiplied profit dollars. Lip-synching gives way to life-synching—the creation of the ultimate crossover artist. But *New York Times* cultural critic Michiko Kakutani warns, "To believe that one can continually assume new identities is to end up having no identity at all."[19]

This is the deathwork culture: Reality is an illusion; truth is a fiction; identity is a persona; all are matters of choice; nothing checks the unfettered self. The deathwork is a world without boundaries. Such we can see in President Clinton, of whom his friends say, "His perception of reality has always been subservient to ambition and desire."[20] Here is the personification of the deathwork logic—reality and truth falling prey to pride and lust.

Sadly, this same celebration of license permeates youth culture today. The challenge of adolescence is not a function of age, but culture. For our teenagers are the heirs of this deathwork. What may be shocking to us as Christian parents is largely taken for granted by our children. This is their world, and this is often how they understand it. We turn next to how the deathwork is expressed and experienced by our teenage children.

CHAPTER EIGHT

A Declaration of Independence

"Who Am I?"

The adolescent journey is about the search for identity. "Who am I?" is the question hidden behind a teen's priorities and behavior. This pursuit is developmentally appropriate, but finding an answer today is fraught with difficulty. The loss of belief in an essential self, as we have seen, empties the self of meaning. Instead, the accepted teenage assumption is that we are only the masks we wear, the personas we project, the brands we buy, the styles we choose.

Bret Easton Ellis in *Glamorama* (1999) throws together a world of compulsive namedropping, an obsession with designer clothing and toned bodies, a fascination with gratuitous gruesome violence, and a cast of vacuous people in a novel where plot is largely beside the point. Panned by critics for its literary value, *Glamorama* nonetheless accurately describes hip-hop youth culture — a world where identity is image.

When journalist Patricia Hersch visited a suburban Virginia middle school, a large banner caught her eye, stating: "IMAGE IS EVERYTHING." She writes, "The school is saturated with the aura of self-conscious posing among middle school students. They walk around hyperalert to what is cool and what is not, who to be like, who is or is not one's friend, what to wear, what to do, how to act. Students are in a state of constant vigilance."[1]

Driving the search for identity is a longing for meaning that is expressed in two questions: *"Where do I find security?"* and *"How do I find significance?"* These two desires dominate the adolescent consciousness. Put differently, teens yearn to "find a home" and "make a name." Or in the parlance of hip-hop, identity is about "finding blood" and "getting big."

Commenting on a photographic essay of American thirteen-year-olds, Charles McGrath observes,

> The really powerful feeling here, the emotion animating almost all these pictures in one way or another, is not so much physical desire as simply the wish to connect: to belong, to fit in. It may not be too much to say that all these kids are looking for surrogate families, for people who will take them in and accept them without question, and what's fascinating is how much the process is reduced to symbols and uniforms.[2]

Or as Patricia Hersch adds, "The wish to be accepted as a 'bro' is an underpinning of the adolescent community of the nineties."[3]

Tom Beaudoin sees the key religious question of youth today as, *"Will you be there for me?"*[4] At its most basic, this is a relational and personal issue rather than a philosophical and abstract one. Born of broken relationships, laced with realism, poignant with need, this question unmasks the fear of abandonment as well as the loss of meaning. It is the cry for an embrace, the passion for intimacy, the longing for fidelity at the deepest levels of the heart—the yearning for love that will not leave in the morning light. Saint Augustine, reflecting on his youth, admits in his *Confessions* that "The single desire that dominated my search for delight was simply to love and to be loved."[5]

This teenage search is primarily worked out among friends—not within the family. At the end of the film mentioned in chapter one, *Disturbing Behavior*, Steve, having abandoned his family, turns to his girl and says, "Let's go home." She responds warily, "Where might that be?" He answers, "Wherever we are."

Thus finding oneself among one's friends becomes an integral part of the teenage years. "Youth is, at once, the loneliest time in a life, and the most conforming," writes Richard Rodriquez.[6] Or as seventeen-year-old Levon says, "Being loved, that's all we want. We're all in this to be loved. . . . We do everything to be loved."[7]

A teen's personal style is the means by which she makes her name and identifies likeminded friends. And in finding friends, she finds security. So it all starts with style — the image she adopts. The school, the mall, the convenience store are the stages on which this performance art of self-creation takes place. "It is in the arena of peers that the struggle for self-definition is waged," writes Hersch.[8]

"I GOT BLOOD"

A "tagger" is an outlaw graffiti artist. Roaming the streets at night with spray-paint cans in hand, these teen vandals leave their mark on buses, subways, overpasses, highway signs, and unguarded walls. Tagging requires a combination of rebellion, creativity, and skill. "Tagging is about getting known. The reason people like to do it is because of the recognition they get. It is like advertising. Like saying, 'I was here,'" says a member of the tagger crew LCK (Loving Crime Kings) in Compton, California.[9]

Tribal Language

Tagging is a metaphor for adolescence — making a name through varieties of rebellious advertising. Adolescence is tribal and every tribe has its tag, such as its own look, sound, and form of escape. Clothes, music, and entertainment are the identity trademarks of adolescent tribalism. To make a generalization, youth culture is unified in terms of its values, but fragmented in its expression. For example, in a typical large high school, school-wide dances are a thing of the past because today's teens listen and dance to very different kinds of music. A hip-hop dancefloor is a distinctly different scene from a heavy-metal mosh pit. It's the same shift we've seen in the change from network to cable television — everyone now has their own special channel.

Within any large high school where uniforms are not enforced there will be variations on ten basic tribes. To be sure, these are stereotypes and there will be regional variations and some blurring of categories between a few of the groups. And it is safe to say that teens do not like someone like me "putting them in a box." Also, some teens will cross over between groups and listen to a wide variety of music. This fact says more about their lack of connectedness to a group than their musical breadth. It can be a symptom of not having found a set group of friends.

Nonetheless, a visit to any high-school cafeteria will reveal the tribal landscape of the adolescent social anthropology. The central point is that youth culture is *tribal* and that this tribalism is expressed in visible *trademarks*.

Here are the basic adolescent tribes:[10]

TRIBE	TAG	MUSIC	APPAREL
Preppy	achievers	pop music	Abercrombie & Fitch or J. Crew
Micro-geeks	nerds	jazz or classic rock	mismatched with graphing calculator
Groovers	drugheads	rave/electronica/ techno/house	torn retro-thrift wear
Motorheads	car jock	metal	Harley-Davidson or Marlboro wear (largely male)
Punk	deviancy	alternative/ grunge	punk
Skaters	extreme sports	Ska	board-sports apparel
Goth	alienation	Goth	black
Hip-hop	street cool	rap	Hilfiger or FUBU (African-American, but also the most dominant tribe across youth culture)
Romantics	eco-hedonism	Phish or Grateful Dead	sixties
Other	Christian, gay, country, Latino, or regional distinctives		

The goal, of course, is to be different, to establish one's own distinctive style. By definition, "cool" is "doing something nobody else is doing." But "cool," Malcolm Gladwell explains, is "a set of dialects, not a language."[11] One's style is found within the safety of a tribe.

Understanding the tribal nature of adolescence is central to understanding the importance of teenage individuality. Tribal fashion is the image of identity. "Pop music," acknowledges MCA-Nashville's president Tony Brown, "is basically fashion."[12] Lilith Fair singer-songwriter Sarah McLachlan makes the point musically in her 1997 hit single, "Building a Mystery." The song is about an exotic teenage Goth who lives in a church, dresses in black, and wears the dreadlocks of a Rastafarian. He is literally "building a mystery and choosing so carefully."[13] McLachlin admits, "It's about being insecure and creating a facade that's more interesting than you think you are. That's me. That's most of the people I know."[14]

The teenage identification with a musical genre may go even deeper than fashion. If fashion emphasizes individuality, music is the marker of identity. The ubiquitous Walkman is as much about self-creation as it is about self-absorption. "Music is life," says Ozzie, a seventeen-year-old high-school senior.[15] Patricia Hersch explains, "What adults don't understand is that music—whether it be rock, heavy metal, or rap—overrides the painful self-consciousness of adolescence; it eases the need for suave interactions and creates an instant community of listeners. . . . Music preferences are a major means of identification."[16]

Music expresses emotions that unite. Let's take a quick look at three musical genres and what they reveal about the youth who are attracted to them.

An Extended Family

The "romantics" are the nineties' variant of the sixties' hippies. Drugs, alcohol, free love, and ecology are blended together in an idealized sense of community. Such is evident in the followers of the Vermont musical group Phish, the heir of the Grateful Dead legacy. More than anything else, Phish is about community. Their 1997 concert in Went, Maine, for instance, drew sixty-seven thousand fans for the three-day festival, creating the second largest community in Maine that August weekend.

As the authors of *The Pharmer's Almanac: The Unofficial Guide to Phish* explain, "For most of us, Phish is not something you hear, it's something you listen to. And going to a concert does not mean pulling into the parking lot just before showtime and rushing to your seat; it's about new friends and old, and being part of an extended family."[17]

What Ben & Jerry's is to ice cream, Phish is to music. Phish promotes northeastern eco-hedonism—a blend of Greenpeace and grass. It is prep-school rock, and it is as much an experience as a musical group, as seventeen-year-old Peach Friedman reflects: "For a band like Phish, hearing the music is only half of it; being part of the community in the audience is just as important. Being there is, for me, a spiritual experience. I've never really believed in God in any organized religion, but I believe in the music."[18]

Celebrating Alienation

The tribe I've identified as "motorheads" listens to heavy metal music. Heavy metal is primarily a male musical genre that centers on themes of alienation and anger. The music emphasizes volume, power, and intensity—what one critic called "the sensory equivalent of war." Sociologist Jeffrey Arnett writes, "Heavy metal songs reaffirm a sense that the world is a hopeless mess, but at the same time the songs comfort them by confirming that they are not alone in their disillusionment."[19]

Metal is a defiant rejection of morality. Its music and performers exemplify and glorify the unrestrained expression of sexual and aggressive impulse. Heavy metal turns alienation into a defiant celebration: "an estrangement from one's culture, a deep loneliness arising from a lack of gratifying emotional connections to others, and cynicism about the ideals and possibilities for life offered by one's culture."[20]

Metal provides the comfort of belonging to a community of cynicism, the worldview of *Beavis and Butthead*. It's a tribe of taboo-breakers who take nothing seriously.

Gold, Guns, and Girls

Finally, we come to the musical genre with the most influence in youth culture today—hip-hop or rap music. Hip-hop chronicler

Nelson George suggests that to "truly understand hip-hop you need a masters degree in sociology, a stint in the joint, and an intimate understanding of African rhythm."[21] Nonetheless, hip-hop has become Mall America's pop style. "Hip-hop is no longer just the Black CNN," writes Charles Aron in *Spin*. "It's also become the unauthorized Bible for white kids everywhere."[22]

"Hip-hop is the rock of today," boasts MC Jean Wyclef.[23] "It is the folk of this generation," says musician Beck.[24] Nelson George explains, "Now we know that rap music, and hip-hop style as a whole, has utterly broken through from its ghetto roots to assert a lasting influence on American clothing, magazine publication, television, language, sexuality, and social policy as well as its obvious presence in records and movies."[25] Indeed, Tommy Hilfiger became the leading apparel company traded on the New York Stock Exchange in 1996 largely due to its embrace of hip-hop.

Hip-hop is hot across racial lines. For the first time ever, in 1998, rap out-sold what previously had been America's top-selling format, country music. These sales are primarily fueled by white kids, who purchase more than 70 percent of hip-hop albums. There is an increasing influence of white rap artists such as the Beastie Boys and Everlast. *The Slim Shady LP,* debut release of Eminen (also known as Marshall Mathers), a white nineteen-year-old rapper from Detroit backed by Dr. Dre, became a pop-hit in 1999 with its angry message: "Life is a bitch, who needs to die, now!"[26]

The central tenets of hip-hop are rebellion, aggression, and materialism. This is pop culture's answer to commodified rebellion. "Hip-hop is perhaps the only art form that celebrates capitalism openly. . . . Rappers make money without remorse," writes *Time's* Christopher Farley.[27] Hip-hop is hoppin' because "materialism replaced spirituality as the definer of life's worth. . . . A voracious appetite for 'goods,' not good."[28] Here is the adolescent dream of gold, guns, and girls.

Hip-hop is not known for its positive message. It reflects the "elemental nihilism" of urban life, which finds a wide appeal in the broader youth culture. "Hip-hop is the rebellious voice of youth. It's what people want to hear," explains MC Jay-Z in *Time's* cover story, "Hip-Hop Nation."[29] "Kids don't want to be like Mike [Michael Jordan] anymore. Their heroes are rappers," claims MC Sean (Puffy) Combs.[30]

These rappers celebrate an in-your-face aggressive attitude toward others. Hip-hop rules the world of youth culture for a reason—it reflects what kids are thinking. Patricia Hersch refers to hip-hop's presence within high schools as the "modern-day Pied Pipers of Bad." For hip-hop, the negative is positive. Expressed academically, it is the "pride of not doing well." Practically, its attitude is, "I do what I want when I want."[31]

So whether it is the angry alienation of metal, the eco-hedonism of Phish, or the rebellious materialism of rap, music frames the choices of youthful identity. The rule of individuality— "To thy own self be true"—is expressed through the rule of identity—"To thy crew be true."

"I GOT BIG"

It is not surprising that hip-hop dominates youth culture. For in the minds of most teenagers, meaning is reduced to money. "If you are doing a story about growing up in LA, you have to show money. That's what it's all about," said a thirteen-year-old boy to photographer Lauren Greenfield. But it was only when she looked at the negatives that she realized the boy had pulled a roll of hundred-dollar bills from his pocket to underscore his point. "Everybody wants to have money," explains rapper G-mo, age twenty. "Everybody wants to be surrounded by beautiful women. Everybody wants the mansion. It's the American dream."[32]

Money buys experience, things, and relationships. It is half of the youth culture's dual emphasis, the other being image. And if adolescence is about identity—the search for security and significance—and identity is reduced to image, then conspicuous consumption becomes the meaning of life and the mall the temple of hyperconsumerism. The deathwork logic is impeccable.

Charles Gandee writes in *Vogue* about teens who spend their days in malls. "To be engulfed in excess, to be enveloped by virtually all of the material temptations our consumer culture taunts us with, is to be transported to a kind of ideal world, where everything is shiny and new and clean and perfect and promising, where reality is replaced by whatever fantasy you might fancy."[33] The reality of kids killing kids for Reebok shoes and Eddie Bauer ski jackets has a cultural context. Behavior always follows beliefs.

But even as consumer nihilism is celebrated in pop, its failure to deliver is all around us. Rapper Foxy Brown (nineteen-year-old Inga Marchand) laments in *Rolling Stone,* "Now I got the platinum Rolie and the [Benz] 600, and I had the illest nigga alive. But it ain't all it seems to be. It's not."[34] Or as rapper Lauryn Hill warns on her Grammy Award-winning album, *The Miseducation of Lauryn Hill,* "You could get the money/You could get the power/But keep your eyes on the final hour."[35]

And yet, the generalized loss of a sense of transcendence has made consumer nihilism the religion of choice among our youth. The American dream is reduced to the American dollar.

DEATHWORK KIDS

American youth largely follow the tenets of the deathwork culture, believing in them without reflection. For this is the world of pop culture — television, music, and film — that has framed our teenagers' consciousness. Moreover, it is the world of their friends.

Half of all teens have what sociologists call a "permissivist worldview." The 1996 survey of American political culture described the "permissivists" as those with the most lenient attitudes toward traditional morality, the most relativistic in their worldview, and among the most hedonistic when negotiating between personal wants and public needs. Permissivists were also the most oriented toward possessive individualism as characterized by such aphorisms as "look out for number one," "nice guys finish last," and "winning isn't everything, it is the only thing."[36]

Religion, and particularly institutional religion, has little place in youth culture. Jeffrey Arnet notes, "For the majority of adolescents growing up in the contemporary West, organized religion has little more relevance to their lives than the horse and carriage have as a mode of transportation." He quotes Brian, age sixteen: "I have no religious anything. I'm not antireligious, but I think that if people like it, that's a personal choice. I choose to believe in myself more than any religion."[37] Where kids are interested in religion, it is usually a syncretistic, nondogmatic, noninstitutional form of neopaganism.[38]

Every study on adolescent behavior or research on the moral beliefs and values of teens makes the same observations: Kids will do whatever they want to do whenever it is in their interest. Truth doesn't play in the picture—more than three out of every four teenagers say there is no absolute moral truth, and four out of five claim that no one can know for certain whether or not they actually know what truth is.[39]

Consider cheating, lying, and stealing. Hersch reports:

> In 1992, a USA Weekend of over 236,000 young people revealed that 25 to 40 percent of teens see nothing wrong with cheating on exams, stealing from employers, or keeping money that isn't theirs. A 1989 Girl Scouts survey of five thousand kids found 65 percent would cheat on an important test. A survey by the Josephson Institute of Ethics in 1992 similarly revealed that 75 percent of high school students admit to cheating.[40]

"Lying is extensive and complex," Hersch continues. "None of the kids give it a second thought. It comes as second nature, not as a means of 'getting away' with something but rather as 'creating space' for their lives they want to live. This behavior is commonplace among their generation: the Josephson Institute of Ethics reports that seven out of ten high school students admit that they lie to parents."[41]

As a rule of thumb, 10 percent of teenagers attempt suicide, 20 percent carry a weapon, 30 percent smoke, 50 percent have used drugs, 50 percent of girls and 85 percent of boys have sex by the time they leave high school, and 90 percent have used alcohol by their senior year. (In 1997, almost one in three twelfth graders, one in four tenth graders, and more than one in ten eighth graders had at least five drinks in a row in the previous two weeks.[42]) What is new is how these same behaviors are emerging among younger and younger children. And here's the clincher—the behaviors of Christian teens and nonChristian teens are virtually identical.[43]

Listen to the voices of teens themselves: "Everyone has sex early. A lot of girls in my grade are not virgins," says Alison, age thirteen. "If you had sex, other kids say, 'Wow, I admire you.' You just try to have sex early to be cool, I guess," says Ari, age thirteen.[44] "By the sophomore year," said James, age sixteen, "sex is common." Or as Amy, also sixteen, says, "It's not a party without alcohol."[45]

In short, kids do not want to be kids, so they act like the adults they see portrayed around them—largely the adults in the celebrity culture of Hollywood. Journalist Peter Carlson observes, "With the decline of traditional family units and communities, we are relying more on celebrities—not grandparents and neighbors—to embody, to make real, to transmit our stories and moral tales."[46]

Los Angeles is the heart of the culture industry. It is the trade-mark capital of adolescence and the harbinger of youth culture. Looking back on growing up in LA, Mijanou, age eighteen, says, "You grow up really fast when you grow up in LA. LA is so fast-moving, and kids really mature at a young age. It seems like everyone is in a rush to be an adult. It's not cool to be a kid."[47]

This is the world of our teenagers—where identity is image, the family is friends, meaning is money, and behavior is "adult." Where does it all lead? To nihilism chic.

CHAPTER NINE

Nihilism Chic

I COME TOO EARLY

As the crowd listened to madman's warning, they reacted with astonishment and disbelief. It seemed so foreign to their Victorian world, all this talk of God being dead. It still seems foreign to many—particularly to parents who are isolated within a Christian subculture. Is this really the youth culture my teenage child inhabits? Aren't these examples of the deathwork culture exaggerations or extremes? Aren't there teenagers who are exceptions to the rule, like the kids in my neighborhood or those who attend my children's youth group?

Yes, there are exceptions. Yes, there are teenagers who resist the pull of youth culture and its consumer-driven liberation of the self. Yes, there are those who keep their spiritual moorings because they have the necessary convictions, character, and community.[1] There are many great teenagers, some of whom I consider my close friends.

The statistics and quotations I cited in the previous chapter are based largely on the experience of middle-class kids—I have not tried to bias the picture by describing the grim socioeconomic realities of inner-city high schools and adolescents.[2] But as the primary issues affecting adolescents are cultural and not geographical or economic, the reality of the deathwork culture is everywhere. It is not simply youth culture. It is *our* culture, but nowhere is it more starkly seen than among our young.

BREAD AND CIRCUS

Where does the deathwork culture—this world that Nietzsche predicted—leave us and our children? With the carnival culture of Hollywood; with the trivial, superficial, and weightless. If nothing is finally real, true, right, or sacred, then nothing can be taken seriously. Everything is a joke; nothing is tragic. This is the deathwork—the culture of talkshow hosts Howard Stern and Jerry Springer, TV shows *Beavis and Butthead* and *South Park*, and films *There's Something About Mary* (1997) and *Baseketball* (1998).

Television defines our cultural reality. It's what Mark Steyn calls "Oprahfication." Steyn observes, "Today, no truly epochal moment in the history of the Republic occurs unless it is validated by her presence."[3] Or as George Gerbner, dean of the Annenberg School of Communication, writes, "Television is the universal curriculum of young and old, the common symbolic environment in which we all live. Its true predecessor is not any other medium but religion—the organic pattern of explanatory symbolism that once animated total communities' sense of reality and value."[4] Historian James Collier adds, "Nothing, perhaps, since the discovery of alcohol has so dramatically altered the nature of human consciousness as television."[5]

Driven by advertising dollars and the accountants' bottom line, television promotes a "want culture" rather than an "ought culture." Critic James Twitchell explains, "Every medium of culture, be it religion, politics, advertising, the law, or psychology is having to live by the rule: Make me feel good or be gone. Entertain or die."[6] The slogan of the age is captured in Nirvana's song "Smells Like Teen Spirit": "Here we are now/Entertain us."[7]

The apathy of such a society is not new. Following an attempted political coup, first-century Roman satirist Juvenal noted, "Now that no one buys our votes, the public has long since cast off its cares; the people that once bestowed commands, consulships, legions and all else, now meddles no more and longs eagerly for just two things—Bread and Circuses."[8] Coups in Rome? Corruption in Washington? Who cares so long as we have a strong economy and a working TV?

But this, Philip Rieff warns, is culture at the verge of collapse. "At the breaking point, a culture can no longer maintain itself as an established span of moral demands. Its jurisdiction contracts; it demands less, permits more. Bread and circuses become confused with right and duty. Spectacle becomes a functional substitute for sacrament." Rieff expands by quoting Carl Jung, "We can hardly realize the whirlwinds of brutality and unchained libido that roared through the streets of Imperial Rome. But we would know that feeling again if ever we understood, clearly and in all its consequences, what is happening under our very eyes."[9] This is the logic of the deathwork culture.

And this is what pervades the carnival culture of adolescence. "'Question Authority' and 'Shit Happens' are more than bumper stickers," states Twitchell. "They are theologies."[10] Vulgarity is thus the *lingua franca* of the deathwork culture and adolescence is its patron saint.

Woodstock '99 was no aberration. "Musically and politically," writes Rob Sheffield in the *Rolling Stone* special report, "Woodstock was the triumph of the bullies, with the fighters winning out over the lovers. Rap-metal gloried in its new clout as the sound of mainstream American youth."[11] Here we witness a youth culture version of the Roman orgy—drugs, sex, and violence. "A raucous frat party flirting with full-blown anarchy."[12] In a reflective essay in *Harper's*, David Samuel writes, "The real causes of the Woodstock riot, if that's what it was, are larger than personal responsibility, or bad music, or poor planning, or greed. The riot is a footnote to a larger story. Thirty years ago something vital and lasting—an idea of the good life and how to live it, what marriage meant, what to eat, what family and community were for, and of who was supposed to take care of the kids when the parents both work—broke apart, and now, thirty years later, that sense of connection, of some overarching narrative frame for our lives, still hasn't been repaired or replaced."[13] Pop nihilism has filled this moral vacuum with bestiality lite.

Yet even the purveyors of youth culture are decrying what they see. *Rolling Stone*'s Erik Hedegaard writes,

> Today the law defines death, with appropriate bluriness, as the cessation of brain function. Though the heart may still throb and the unknowing bone marrow creates new cells, no man's history can out live his brain. And so this is what is found at the most furious moment of a *Jerry Springer Show*, when reason and civility are at their most distant remove: cultural brain death, the end of the dream we used to call America.[14]

Cultural brain death. Life seems to continue but without any basis for meaning or morals. We walk the streets of Imperial Rome once more. Harvard philosopher Sissela Bok points out, "Nietzsche, who celebrated the Romans as the strongest, noblest people who ever lived . . . has no rival among philosophers in extolling cruelty as central, liberating, and exhilarating in human culture."[15] The news report of two brothers, age thirteen and fifteen, repeatedly raping their eight-year-old half-sister, which they claimed to have learned on the *Jerry Springer Show*, should come as no surprise.[16]

Beliefs have consequences in behavior. The death of God leads to the death of man. As Fyodor Dostoyevsky put it, "Humanness is only a habit, a product of civilization. It may completely disappear."[17] This is the lesson being learned again and again in elementary, middle, and high schools across the country.

THE CULTURE OF DEATH

The realities of middle-class kids today are stark and grim. "Nearly all of the kids killed in multiple school shootings since 1996 came from small suburban and rural communities. Watching the myth of sylvan innocence go down in a blaze of gunfire has been a profoundly discouraging experience. There are no safe places left," Randall Sullivan laments in the pages of *Rolling Stone*.[18]

Newsweek reports an epidemic of heroin use among teens in the wealthy Dallas suburb of Plano: "Though the local schools had their share of burnouts and stoners, they weren't the ones who discovered the drug first. Instead, it was a core group of wealthier cool kids, preppies, and jocks, who started sniffing and smoking the brown powder at parties."[19] A seventeen-year-old overdose victim who taught Sunday school at a local church told the magazine, "In the beginning I was so against it. I was raised in a real strong Christian home, and I'm strong-willed. But once you're around it every day, it becomes pretty ordinary. Then you get curious, and you think it's not a big deal to do it one time."[20]

On March 1, 1989, a group of fifteen white high-school athletes from Glen Ridge, New Jersey, lured a mentally retarded teenage neighbor into a basement where they repeatedly raped her and stuck a broomstick and baseball bat into her vagina. It was reported after their arrest that "none actually believed that what had been done to the girl was wrong or degenerate. Gross, yes. But certainly not immoral—or illegal."[21] All of the boys came from apparently stable families with two parents who were regular churchgoers and active in the civic affairs of the community.

On May 24, 1997, in the rural town of Gloversville, New York, two sixteen-year-olds tied a retiree in his late seventies to an easy chair and tipped him forward with his face pushed into the floor. Cushions, cloths, and an old vacuum cleaner were piled on top of him so that he would slowly asphyxiate. What was particularly shocking about this murder was that as many as thirty students at Gloversville High School knew about it, but no one said a word to a grownup. It was only by happenstance that the police discovered the body.[22]

On April 20, 1999, in the Denver suburb of Littleton, Colorado, two high-school seniors entered Columbine High School during lunch armed with bombs and automatic weapons. They killed twelve students and a teacher and injured twenty-three others before turning their guns on themselves. The Littleton massacre galvanized the attention of the nation and the world. But after the tears were shed and the dead buried, few answers were forthcoming.

The rash of copycat threats and killings that followed the Littleton tragedy in schools across North America made parents and teachers realize that no neighborhood was safe and no school immune. In an opinion piece for the *Washington Post*, economist

Robert J. Samuelson wrote, "We search for meaning. But the explanation, if any, of the Columbine slaughter lies at the juncture of the dark side of human nature and the drift of our culture."[23]

Or as Peggy Noonan wrote two days after the shooting in the *Wall Street Journal,*

> The kids who did this are responsible. They did it. They killed. But they came from a place and time, and were yielded forth by a culture. What walked into Columbine High School Tuesday was the culture of death. This time it wore black trench coats. Last time it was children's hunting gear. Next time it will be some other costume, but it will still be the culture of death. . . . The boys who did the killing, the famous Trench Coat Mafia, inhaled too deep the ocean in which they swam.[24]

Young people are increasingly citizens of an autonomous country. Even if they live at home, by the age of eleven their spirits dwell elsewhere. Pop culture provides teenagers with fantasies of an authority-free world, from the slick pages of the Abercrombie & Fitch catalog to the violent heat of the mosh pit.

Writing about the nihilistic film *Kids* (1995), Jon Pareles remarks, "Old-fashioned tormented teenagers, the ones who were desperate for meaning and direction, are giving way to the dead-eyed kids who don't bother to report a murder. Numbed by drugs and mass culture, restless but affectless, they don't feel much beyond immediate physical lusts."[25] William Finnegan chronicles in *Cold New World,* "The ideological void left by consumerism tends to get filled . . . by apathy, frustration, hedonism, nihilism, or an excess of the emotional detachment known as cool."[26] These are Nietzsche's children.

The challenges facing parents seem overwhelming. The nihilistic undertow of the deathwork culture seems to drown the efforts of even the most conscientious mother or father. Yet unless we are fully aware of what we are facing as parents of teenagers, we will not be likely to take the necessary steps. What, then, should we do? What are our responsibilities? What should be our priorities? We turn to them next in part three.

THE PRIORITIES OF CHRISTIAN PARENTING

CHAPTER TEN

Followers First

PRIORITY:
Be Apprentices of Jesus

OUR SPIRITUAL RESPONSIBILITY

What, then, is ours to do as Christian parents? In the following chapters I will suggest ten priorities. There is nothing magic in the number, and much more could be said. The ten items are not recipes, how-tos, or techniques; nor are we guaranteed "perfect" children as a result of following them prayerfully. But by God's grace, in doing so we may be remembered as Christ-like parents.

Together these guidelines suggest necessary aspects of a relationship with our teenage children. They cover Christ's life and lordship as the foundation for our influence with our teenagers, the importance of understanding and connecting with our sons and daughters, the basis of our authority, the priority of beliefs, our need to respect our children's freedom, and the power of their friends.

The premise underlying this book could be summarized in one sentence: *Christ-like parenting involves treating our children as Jesus treats us.* It is both that simple and that demanding. Parenting is the supreme case study of the state of our heart, and no one knows this better than our teenager. As C. S. Lewis reminds us, "Those who leave their manners behind them when they come home from the dance or the sherry party have no real courtesy even there. They were merely aping those who had."[1]

The parenting task, then, is spiritual—it's more about who we are than what we do. It cannot be accomplished in our own strength or through our own natural inclinations; unconditional love never originates in us but rather is channeled through us. Thus parenting begins with the transformation of the heart of the parent who is an apprentice of Jesus. There is no other basis for influencing teens to life in the kingdom.[2]

Parenting is a form of teaching. Educator Parker Palmer gets to the heart of parenting well: "Good teaching cannot be reduced to technique; good teaching comes from the identity and integrity of the teacher."[3] The next two chapters explore the importance of a parent's private identity and public integrity.

Warning — "Christian" Parents Ahead

Today it is a spiritual risk for a child to have so-called "Christian" parents, for what counts as "Christian" within many families is often a long way from Christ. And no one can blunt the force of the gospel like a parent, as we can see in the lives of many leading atheists and agnostics who throughout the years have come from Christian homes. For example, at a recent Veritas Forum, Berkeley professor Philip Johnson was addressed by an audience member who said that he had been raised by atheist parents before coming to faith. Johnson responded, "Ah, but I was raised by nominal Christians, which is far more difficult." Nominal faith often works like a vaccine to genuine faith—just enough half-truths to turn one off to the Truth.

For a contemporary example, take pop diva Tori Amos, the daughter of a North Carolina Methodist minister. She describes her music as a "mission to expose the dark side of Christianity." As Steven Daly writes for *Rolling Stone*, "Compared with the Amos *oeuvre*, Madonna's blasphemous stunts look positively devout; and when this little minister's daughter starts exorcising the 'shame' of her 'Victorian Christian' upbringing, she makes *soidisant* Satanist Marilyn Manson seem cartoonish and ineffectual."[4]

Historically, PKs ("preacher's kids") have only been bested by MKs ("missionary's kids") for sheer rebellion. Here I speak with some authority. As the son of a missionary surgeon, I spent my adolescent years attending a missionary boarding school where PKs and MKs ruled the roost. Twenty-five years later some of my classmates are still bitter over their parents' gross hypocrisy and coercive moralism. Sadly, the public face of professional Christianity too often masks the quality of relationships behind closed doors.

Christian parents face two specific dangers that undercut the influence of the gospel in the lives of their children. The first, hypocrisy, is about what the teenager observes in the home; the second, moralism, is about what is imposed on the teenager.

Behind Closed Doors

Hypocrisy is one of the greatest dangers of the Christian life. What was prevalent among religious leaders in Jesus' day is an even greater danger for followers of Christ living under the conditions of modern life. Jesus could have been speaking for many teens living within so-called Christian homes when He said about the Pharisees, "They talk a good line, but they don't live it. They don't take it into their hearts and live it out in their behavior. It's all spit-and-polish veneer" (Matthew 23:3-5, MSG).

The Greek word *hypocrisis* is used in the New Testament twenty-five times, and over half of the verses are found in the book of Matthew. This is not surprising as this gospel was written for the Jewish community, which was living within a religious subculture. The roots of the word come from the Greek theater and originally the term had no negative connotations. Instead, it was used to describe a person giving a declamation or playing a part on the stage.

But Jesus used the word to mean a person who play-acts a role of virtue or spirituality while not actually possessing the private reality expressed in the public performance. Unfortunately, this is an apt description of many of us parents today. At home we feel the liberty to "let our hair down," to go about in our "at-home fashion," to treat others with the anonymity afforded "behind closed doors." But it is here, Jesus warned, that the reality of our lives is truly revealed.

When Jesus addressed hypocrites He used the sharpest language recorded in Scripture—"fools," "blind guides," "sons of hell," "brood of vipers." No other sin was so sternly denounced, for no other sin so undermines the message of the gospel. In Luke 12:1 he said, "Beware of the leaven of the Pharisees, which is hypocrisy" (NKJV). We best take the issue seriously, for Jesus did. In Matthew 23:3-12 He describes three characteristics of hypocrites.

Fundamental Dishonesty

First, Jesus states that hypocrites lack honesty: "Do not do what they do, for they do not practice what they preach" (verse 3). His words remind me of the saying that "All people have two beliefs; one that they say they believe and one that they practice. The one that they practice is the one they truly believe."

Surely one of the great errors of discipleship is the notion that becoming a Christian is merely a matter of mental assent— knowing and agreeing with doctrinal truth without acting any differently. Jesus' half-brother James put a dent into such notions of grace. He warns,

> Do I hear you professing to believe in the one and only God, but then observe you complacently sitting back as if you had done something wonderful? That's just great. Demons do that, but what good does it do them? Use your heads! Do you suppose for a minute that you can cut faith and works in two and not end up with a corpse on your hands? (James 2:18-19, MSG)

Parents are hypocrites if in their child's eyes they look the part, say all the right words, go to all the right functions, but fail to walk under Jesus' authority and to embody the reality of His love within the home. There will be no influence where there is no integrity. The issue is not perfection but the pattern of our lives.

No Helping Hand

Second, Jesus observes that hypocrites are not helpful: "They tie up heavy loads and put them on men's shoulders, but they themselves are not willing to lift a finger to move them" (Matthew 23:4). The problem is not only with the inconsistency of their own lives, but with their attitude toward others. They place a heavy trip on those around them with all their talk about rules and prohibitions. But they don't help those who can't handle it. At heart, hypocrites lack empathy—the sense that we're in this together, that we share a common responsibility to help each other in our spiritual pilgrimage.

When I've talked to my teens about their entertainment choices, I don't frame the discussion in terms of age or maturity, such as, "You're just too young," as if the age of seventeen or twenty-one automatically qualifies one for "adult" entertainment. Rather, the question I ask them is the same question I ask myself when considering a film or CD: "Will it help us become more or less sensitive to the reality of Christ in our lives?"

What we ask of our teens must be seen as what we ask of ourselves. We are not the arbitrary authority; we are together under God's commands. And we are to seek the help of our teens in our spiritual pilgrimage just as we seek to help them.

No Humility

The third characteristic of hypocrites is that they lack humility— they look down on others and assume a posture of moral or intellectual superiority. We are told in Luke 18 that the Pharisee prayed, "God, I thank you that I am not like other men—robbers, evildoers, adulterers—or even like this tax collector" (verse 11). We might update the prayer, "I am glad I'm not like my punk teenage son or my Goth teenage daughter."

Hypocrites are into impression management with the clothes they wear, the titles they insist on, the places of honor they demand. Everything is "done for men to see" (Matthew 23:5). Because their authority is based on appearances, they cannot bear the thought of being on an equal spiritual footing with others. Jesus warns in Matthew 23:8, "But you are not to be called 'Rabbi,' for you have only one Master and you are all brothers"—you are all in this together. Spiritually, parents and children are brothers and sisters in Christ.

When parents are into the "impression management" of their children, they reveal their own priorities, as I witnessed recently. I was called to help after a seventeen-year-old daughter had been found to be drinking, taking drugs, and running with the wrong crowd. The Christian parents cracked down and sent her away from her friends to another city, where she promptly tried to commit suicide. The first words the parents said about the situation were, "She has brought great shame on the family." More than anything, this statement exposes this family's priority of "looking good" among their friends and neighbors. Their concern was less for their daughter than their reputation.

Modern society downplays character; it attempts to compensate with public relations—the numerous ways we seek to control how others perceive us. But both the Scriptures and human history show the lie in such pretense. We are our secrets, not our spin. What is true on the inside is what is finally true before God, whatever the short-term appearances.

Humility is neither the way of the world nor the hypocrite. But only when we forego hypocrisy and adopt the posture of humility will our teenage children listen. For then—and only then—our words will stem from the integrity of our lives.

Life Under Surveillance

If the first obstacle to influence is the hypocrisy our children observe within our homes, then the second is parental preoccupation with our children's behavior. A repeated theme throughout this book is that *behavior is not the battle*. If our focus as parents is controlling behavior, then our success will only be as wide as the sphere of our constraint. As our teens get older, we will need to impose ever greater measures of surveillance.

A recent cover story of the *Washington Post* reads, "Children Under Surveillance: When Parents' Trust Wears Out, Some Resort to Spying on Their Teens." The article gives an account of parents who have resorted to police procedures to spy on their children. It describes the use of phone and computer taps, private investigators, sprays for detecting drugs, home drug urinalysis and hair sample kits, video cameras, computerized analysis of driving patterns, and breath analyzers for alcohol. Drug-sniffing dogs are hired like Terminex, ChemLawn, or Merry Maids to make monthly checkups on the teens.

Parents lament the action. One says, "I felt absolutely filthy. It's the last thing I wanted to do—turn into the KGB in our own house."[5] Bolts and alarms are placed on her teens' windows, locking them in their rooms each night like common criminals.

This is the logical conclusion of parents whose concern is control rather than influence. Gregory Bodenhamer teaches such draconian measures to desperate parents and speaks simultaneously of "creating a loving relationship with your adolescent."[6] But this is not possible through such means. Rather, parents who pursue such strategies open a Pandora's box, with each step of surveillance further undermining a future reconciliation with their children.

Condemnation and coercion lower the potential for our loving influence with our sons and daughters. E. Stanley Jones, Methodist missionary to India, observes: "Suppose a parent would dictate to the child minutely everything he is to do during the day. The child would be stunted under that regime. The parent must guide in such a manner, and to the degree, that autonomous character, capable of making right decisions for itself, is produced. God does the same."[7] In short, the prodigal son was not locked down.

Whether within the home or church, moralism puts the emphasis on behavior, not the heart. Moreover, moralism places a premium on actions that can be readily seen rather than attitudes that can remain largely hidden. Thus a teen's sex, drugs, and cigarettes trump the pride, greed, and envy of parents.

Jesus' concern, in contrast, is our motives. His interest is our heart—our beliefs and loves. William Wilberforce, the English nineteenth-century evangelical leader, writes, "Indeed, it is the heart which constitutes the man. External actions derive their character and meaning from the motives and dispositions of the heart, of which they are but indicators. . . . A distinguishing glory of Christianity is not to rest satisfied with superficial appearances but to correct the motives and purify the heart."[8]

But, of course, concern for the heart not only speaks to our priorities in parenting but to who we are as parents. We cannot give what we do not have. C. S. Lewis writes of education, "No generation can bequeath to its successor what it has not got; . . . if we are skeptical we shall teach only skepticism to our pupils, if fools only folly, if vulgar only vulgarity, if saints sanctity, if heroes heroism. . . . Nothing which was not in the teacher can flow from them to the pupils."[9] As with teaching, so it is with parenting.

THE REALITY OF JESUS

The choice before parents today is Christ or Nietzsche, life or death: "I have set before you life and death, blessings and curses. Now choose life, so that *you and your children* may live and that you may love the LORD your God, listen to his voice, and hold fast to him. For the LORD is your life" (Deuteronomy 30:19-20, emphasis added). True parenting begins with the parents' conscious daily appropriation of the transformative life of Jesus.

"Remain in Me"

Parenting is learning to live out the life of Jesus before our children in the totality of our lives. Living in the reality of Jesus is not something we will learn from the latest self-help paperback. Rather we learn it from Jesus Himself as we apprentice ourselves to Him.

We are to be Jesus in the life of our child. "Impossible!" you say. Precisely. Following Jesus is not primarily about doctrine or behavior but about life—appropriating Jesus' life in our lives. Lip service is like lip-synching, and kids will not be fooled. Oswald Chambers states bluntly, "You cannot imitate the disposition of Jesus; it is either there or it is not."[10]

This is the often overlooked point of Jesus' statement, "I am the vine; you are the branches. If a man remains in me and I in him, he will bear much fruit; apart from me you can do nothing" (John 15:5). The point of this passage is not the fruit, but the life—the life that is found in the vine.

Jesus tells us how we can rely on His spiritual resources for our life. He says, "If you remain in me and my words remain in you, ask whatever you wish, and it will be given you" (John 15:7). Remaining is Jesus' metaphor of the source of our most ultimate confidence and trust in life. Dallas Willard adds, "Where we spontaneously look for 'information' on how to live shows what we believe in and who we have confidence in."[11]

Some people *remain* in Regis and Kathy Lee or Oprah. Many *remain* in their therapists. Others *remain* in themselves. Our teens tend to *remain* in their peers. As followers of Jesus we are to *remain* in Him. "To trust the real person Jesus is, to have confidence in him in every dimension of our real life, to believe that he is right about and adequate to everything," Willard observes.[12] To the degree that such trust is not our belief, the source of our life remains in something other than Christ. The fruit of our lives will then point back to that source, and not to Christ.

Our children are looking for the reality of Jesus in their Christian parents. We have little to offer as parents if Jesus is not our passion, our reliance, and our life.

Living and Loving

A few years ago I was asked to give an address to a college prep school as if it were my dying advice on the last day of my life. In the audience would be my children, who were students at the school. After much reflection, I decided on the following: If you learn how to love, you will have learned how to live. But the opposite is probably closer to the truth: If you learn how to live, you will love. This is the life Jesus brings to His followers.

How is it done? Does wearing a bracelet with the letters WWJD ("What would Jesus do?") produce a loving heart?[13] Does regular attendance at a Bible study produce a loving heart? Does participation in a men's rally produce a loving heart? Helpful? Maybe. Adequate? No. Jesus suggests three steps to appropriating His life in our lives—apprenticeship, ascertaining, and asking.

First, we are to "remain" in Him. The call is to a lifelong apprenticeship whose goal is to "learn from Jesus to live my life as he would live my life if he were I. I am not necessarily trying to do everything he did, but I am learning to do everything I do in the manner that he did all that he did."[14]

Second, we are to listen—"my words [are to] remain in you." As Jesus says in John 8:31-32, "If you dwell in my word, you are really my apprentices. And you will know the truth and the truth will liberate you."[15] It is through listening to His words that we ascertain His mind.

Third, we are to ask—"ask whatever you wish, and it will be given you." "Remaining" is about the dynamic of an ongoing relationship with Jesus: being with, listening to, and talking over what we are doing together. In the process we are changed from the inside out; we receive the resources of the kingdom so that our life reflects His life.

"Whoever claims to live in him must walk as Jesus did," John writes (1 John 2:6). The measure of our walk is seen in the way we treat others, and the bottom line is love. "If anyone obeys his word, God's love is truly made complete in him" (1 John 2:5). "God is love. Whoever lives in love lives in God, and God in him" (1 John 4:16). Spiritual reality is measured by our relationships.

The key is to aim at the heart and its transformation, for love will be our behavior when our lives remain in Jesus. We tend to focus on the fruit but should focus on the tree—on beliefs, not behavior. We do not aim to control behavior through moralism, but to change the inner castle of the soul. Then behavior is not the result of a performance, but a Person.[16] We must be able to say like Paul, "Follow my example, as I follow the example of Christ" (1 Corinthians 11:1).

The task of Christian parents is to love our child as Jesus loves our child. Jesus commands, "Love each other as I have loved you" (John 15:12). And love is the fruit that remains. "I chose you and appointed you," Jesus says to Christian parents, "to go and bear fruit—fruit that will last" (John 15:16).

If we keep this task foremost in our minds we will stay on our knees in a posture of true humility. Here we will avoid the sin of hypocrisy—of standing over our teen. Here we will refrain from a high-hover mode of control. For here, humbled before God, will we engage in true parenting, which is not something we can do in our own strength. Anything less makes a mockery of what parenting demands and what our children deserve.

Tori Amos grew up with a Christianity that was hypercritical and moralistic. She heard little of the priority of the heart or the importance of soul-work. It was outside-in, behavior-oriented parenting. "The problem with Christianity," she told *Rolling Stone*, "is they think everything is about outside forces, good and evil. With Christianity there's not a lot of inner work encouraged. . . . I think a lot of kids are starving in high school—they want tools to do the inner work."[17] Kids know the real from the fake. Parenting begins with the state of our heart.

CHAPTER ELEVEN

"The Whole World Is Watching"

P R I O R I T Y :
*Live Our Life with Integrity for
That Which Matters*

"HASKELL, IT'S REAL!"

In the midst of the turbulent events of the summer of 1968, film director Haskell Wexler made *Medium Cool* (1969), a movie that explores the relationship between the media's portrayal of reality with actual events. The plot concerns a Chicago TV cameraman and his sound technician who are sent to cover the turmoil and riots that followed the assassinations of Martin Luther King, Jr. and Robert F. Kennedy. The actors mingle in and out of what is actually happening, blurring the boundaries of the film's story and the national crisis unfolding on the streets of America.

Eventually the cameraman finds himself covering the 1968 Democratic Convention in Chicago with the corresponding violent confrontation on the streets outside between the students and the combined forces of the Chicago Police Department and the Illinois National Guard. The encounter is an epic struggle between adult authority and youthful rebellion. Wexler's actors walk among the ensuing brutality, dodging police in riot gear and soldiers with bayonets fixed to their loaded rifles.

A crucial turning point in the clash comes when military

armored personnel carriers roll against a sea of students sitting in protest—the sixties' version of Tiananmen Square. The students shout confidently to the television cameras, "The whole world is watching!" But then the police order the filming crews to leave. The students, fearing what will happen when the protection of media coverage ceases, shout, "ABC, don't go!" Just then the police let off rounds of tear-gas canisters. One falls at the feet of Wexler, who is still filming his actors as they wander through the smoke-filled commotion. The camera jiggles and the viewer hears off camera, "Look out, Haskell, it's real!" The scene ends.

STORIES OF HOME

Another story is unfolding in each of our homes, the story of parents—sometimes one, sometimes married. Wandering in and out of the narration are the children. By example they are taught how to treat others and what is important in life. Where personal peace and affluence are the dream—if not the reality—the children will thereby shape their priorities. Where condemnation is the pattern, so will the children learn to treat others. "If Christian parents want their children to be Christ-like," writes Dick Keyes in *True Heroism in a World of Celebrity Counterfeits,* "the parents' lives must be 'good stories.'"[1] These are not daytime soaps or staged docu-dramas but real stories with real consequences.

Two of the deepest desires that motivate us as people made in the image of God are wanting to be loved and wanting to make a difference. For an adolescent, the same desires dominate what is important and define what is meaningful. Dallas Willard writes, "Meaning is not a luxury for us. It is a kind of spiritual oxygen, we might say, that enables our souls to live."[2] The Gospels express this as, "What kind of deal is it to get everything you want but lose yourself? What could you ever trade your soul for?" (Matthew 16:26, MSG). Or as New York University professor Neil Postman observes, "Without air, our cells die. Without a story, our selves die."[3]

We learn the first lessons of meaning at our parent's knee. As Keyes writes, "A child looks out at the many options that life offers, and compares stories. He or she wants to know what to do with freedom, with the open-endedness of the story."[4] As we discussed in the last chapter, children learn the story of relationship and love from the private home-life of their mothers and fathers. In this chapter we will look at how the parents' public work-world influences how children learn the story about what is important to do with their lives. We turn to this second aspect of a parent's story—the measure of a parent's treasure.

"WHAT DOES YOUR FATHER DO?"

A large part of my summers growing up in Korea were spent at Boy Scout camps held at a Nike-Hercules missile test site on the western shore of South Korea. Each autumn U.S. soldiers would be there shooting down drones launched from the nearby Kunsan Air Force Base. The paramilitary flavor of Boy Scouts was in full regalia as each morning we lined up for the raising of the flag and each night we were put to bed by "Taps."

Our small troop of missionary Boy Scouts was wide-eyed at the sights and smells—this was the closest many had ever come to being in America. But as I mixed with the military kids, I was amazed at how few knew anything about what their fathers did for a living. It wasn't that their dads' postings were top secret, only that the kids didn't know or seem to care.

It wasn't just the military kids, however. Many of my missionary classmates never had an appreciation for nor a commitment to the calling that had brought their parents to the mission field. But this was never the case in our family. Together each morning we would pray for Dad's surgical procedures. Then when we were old enough, my sisters and I accompanied my father on his 6:30 A.M. medical rounds at the hospital and watched surgery from a stool. At times we were introduced to dying cancer patients our own age.

We were brought into the public world of our parents. Their lives became the stage on which we saw them play out their priorities and passions. It was here that we learned the themes of their story—what occupied their time and talents and what they deemed important. It wasn't a philosophy class or a religious discourse, but our first course in life.

MEASURE OF ONE'S TREASURE

The search for meaning is the subject of Ecclesiastes, an ancient book with a modern message. Philosopher Peter Kreeft writes, "Ecclesiastes is the one book in the Bible that modern man needs most to read, for it is Lesson One, and the rest of the Bible is Lesson Two, and modernity does not heed Lesson Two because it does not heed Lesson One."[5]

Solomon, the writer of Ecclesiastes, poses a challenge to his reader that Nietzsche later made: "Try to find meaning in a world without God. To do so is a wild goose chase. But I dare you, prove me wrong." Human nature being what it is, Solomon argues, there are not an infinite variety of avenues through which people explore meaning.

What makes Solomon's argument powerful is its down-to-earth character. His is not a scholarly treatise on alternative worldviews but a practical exploration of our everyday lives. Nietzsche said succinctly, "Metaphysics are in the street."[6] Like Solomon, he knew that the final problems of the human condition are not found in a book as much as in our living. Every parent's life is a Technicolor illustration of this fact.

Ecclesiastes examines five lifestyle choices that shape most of human endeavor. These are the dominant myths of advertising; the promises of fulfillment offered in a world that views God as irrelevant to happiness and wholeness. Each has its strongest attraction at particular times in our lives. Each has a dominant cultural and geographical address. Each appeals to our varying strengths and temperaments. They move from that which is most purchasable and popular to that which is most esoteric and elitist.[7]

1. Pleasure/Los Angeles/Entertainment

Pleasure is the lifestyle promoted by Hollywood, the epicenter of youth culture. Pleasure is the most popular, the most American, and the most amenable to consumerism. Whether derived from legal or illegal sources, refined or crude practices, the fundamental approach to living is the same. As Solomon writes, "I tried cheering myself with wine, and embracing folly. . . . I denied myself nothing my eyes desired; I refused my heart no pleasure" (Ecclesiastes 2:3,10).

We can see its pursuit clearly among students whose theme could be characterized as "having a good time." College administrators struggle to control binge drinking and resort to all sorts of measures to restrict alcohol consumption. But they have done little to address the latent hedonism that lies behind the behavior.

Pleasure for pleasure's sake has a darker side, as seen in the sensation-seeking impulses of adolescence. Sociologist Jeffrey Jensen Arnett writes, "In both automobile accidents and crime, sensation seeking plays a key role—adolescents drive recklessly and commit crimes in greater proportion than the rest of the population at least partly because they find these activities *exciting* and *fun*."[8]

Take, for example, Rafal Zielinski's film, *Fun* (1994), the story of two fourteen-year-old girls, Bonnie and Hillary. They meet by chance on their way to school and spend the day in wild, anti-social behavior, culminating in the killing of an elderly woman. Not heartless or crazy, Hillary and Bonnie are simply teens acting on their beliefs. "We just did the baddest thing in the whole world and I feel great," Hillary admits at the end of the day. Bonnie explains later to the prison counselor, "I never do what I don't have to do unless it's fun. Fun is the meaning of life."

2. Power/New York/Business

"Power," claims Helen Gurney Brown, editor of *Cosmopolitan*, "is the ultimate aphrodisiac." Solomon writes, "I amassed silver and gold for myself, and the treasure of kings and provinces. I acquired men and women singers, and a harem as well—the delights of the heart of man. I became greater by far than anyone in Jerusalem" (Ecclesiastes 2:8-9). His words could have been taken straight from the rap lyrics of Sean "Puffy" Combs or Master P.

This is the lifestyle of Sherman McCoy, the self-acclaimed "Master of the Universe" in Tom Wolfe's *The Bonfire of the Vanities*. Today, when Wall Street brokers and other New Yorkers finish work they turn to white-collar boxing, the latest fitness craze that's more about power than getting into shape. As one film executive gushes, "It's more than addictive, it's indescribable. It's the power involved, the danger."[9]

More than simply wealth, power is the desire to control. "If I had a servant in my employ who, when I asked him for a cup of cold water, brought instead the world's costliest wines blended in a chalice, I would dismiss him; for true pleasure consists not in getting my wine, but in getting my way," observes Søren Kierkegaard.[10]

Power in the streets is often found at the end of a gun. Teens carry these weapons as a tool of the drug trade or for protection from others; most often, however, they pack metal as a symbol of power. "Who's going to mess with a pistol?" asks a neighbor of Travis Savoy, a quiet fourteen-year-old Maryland youth charged with multiple murders.[11]

Fame and fear go hand in hand. As a Southeast Los Angeles youth explains, "We'd rather be known by putting in work into our gang, you know, by going and shooting people. We'd rather be known that way, the violent way, than by, 'Oh, I saw your name graffitied on the wall.' When you are hated by a lot of people, you're known."[12] The high is not the stolen Eddie Bauer coat, but getting one's way.

3. Helping Others/Washington/Politics or Philanthropy

Altruism is one of the most seductive forms of seeking meaning—it seems so intrinsically noble. Solomon writes, "I saw the tears of the oppressed—and they have no comforter; power was on the side of their oppressors—and they have no comforter" (Ecclesiastes 4:1). Whether the desire is to fight oppression, restore justice, or alleviate suffering—whether it's endangered rain forests or Tibetan independence—helping others can be a powerful personal source of meaning.

Of course, haunting the "do-gooder" in a world without God is the question, "Why bother?" Albert Camus poses this issue in *The Plague,* the story of Dr. Bernard Rieux as he works doggedly against the ravaging effects of bubonic plague. Rieux's answer is that he's simply doing his job: "There's no question of heroism in all this. It's a matter of common decency. That's an idea which may make some people smile, but the only means of fighting a plague is—common decency."[13] We instinctively fight evil, even when we don't know why.

When we don't know the source of meaning, helping others turns into the blind leading the blind. When wealth does not satisfy, alleviating poverty is no answer. If power is impotent, then empowerment is a dead end. As Solomon asks, if life has no meaning, then why preserve life itself? If nature is meaningless, why work for sustainability?

4. Spirituality/Santa Fe/Self-Help or Therapy

As we have seen, spirituality has wide appeal today. And yet these new forms of spirituality rarely move one beyond the worship of one's own ego. Angels, astrology, and channeling naturally devolve into spiritualized pleasure and power by other means.

Moreover, worshiping the impersonal, amoral god of nature, Solomon observes, ends in synthesizing good and evil. "Consider what God has done: Who can straighten what he has made crooked? When times are good, be happy; but when times are bad, consider: God has made the one as well as the other. Therefore, a man cannot discover anything about his future" (Ecclesiastes 7:13-14). Here Solomon is not referring to the God of the Bible, but to the "God" of conventional naturalistic religion.

"All of life's riddles are answered in the movies," claims Steve Martin in *Grand Canyon* (1991). The characters in his film, like many contemporary seekers, look instead to nature. Trying to make sense of their senseless lives, Simon and Mack stand before the grandeur of the Grand Canyon. Simon remarks, "It makes you feel like a gnat on the back of a cow in a field you pass at seventy miles an hour."

Our momentary problems seem to pale in significance before the immensity of nature. Yet standing before its impersonal, random forces—for all the splendor—does not address our longing for love and meaning. "More and more of our young are finding that the accidental life is scarcely worth living," observes Neil Postman.[14]

5. Knowledge/Boston/Education

Finally, Solomon turns to the pursuit of knowledge. "I applied myself to the understanding of wisdom, and also of madness and folly, but I learned that this, too, is a chasing after the wind. For with much wisdom comes much sorrow; the more knowledge, the more grief" (Ecclesiastes 1:17-18).

The United States is today's postsecondary education super-power. We have nearly thirty-seven hundred colleges and universities that enroll 14.5 million people, or about a quarter of the college students in the world.[15] Yet for all of the academy's size and status, it has lost a unifying purpose—besides size and status. Within the staid, ivy-covered halls, academic fiefdoms war over dollars and influence.

Many reasons lie behind the hyperspecialization and fragmentation of knowledge that characterizes the modern university—some historical, some political, some economic.[16] But the widespread abandonment of truth within the academy has led to a studied effort to avoid asking the big questions. Those who do, like Christian scholars, are derided by Richard Rorty as "metaphysical prigs" prone to "philosophical machismo" likely to encourage the fundamentalism and fanaticism of Shiites, Marxists, and Nazis.[17]

As a consequence, scholars know more and more about less and less. As Kreeft observes from his years of teaching within the university culture, "It knows more about the little things and less about the big things. It knows more about every thing and less about Everything."[18]

And yet big questions remain. Frustrated with philosopher Bertrand Russell's reluctance to address the issues of human existence and destiny, novelist Somerset Maugham wrote,

> It may be that, as he says, philosophy doesn't offer or attempt to offer a solution to the problems of human destiny; it may be that it mustn't hope to find an answer to the practical problems of life; for philosophers have other fish to fry. But who then will tell us whether there is any sense in living, and whether human existence is anything but a tragic—no, tragic is too noble a word—whether human existence is anything but a grotesque mischance."[19]

Great learning, it seems, has the tendency to leave one with more questions than answers. There is frequently more wisdom in the common person than a conceited scholar. Pascal notes, "Pious scholars are rare."[20]

True Allegiance

Solomon encourages his readers to think of other possible lifestyle options, challenging us with his conclusion that "all is vanity." Pursued without reference to God, meaning cannot be found. The great twentieth-century existentialist Jean-Paul Sartre admits the same: "The existentialist thinks it very distressing that God does not exist, because all possibility of finding value in a heaven of ideas disappears with Him."[21] The options are God or nothingness.

And yet this same sentiment, which many Christian parents affirm for an hour on Sunday mornings, is belied by their priorities the rest of the week. It is many a Christian father or mother who on bended knee says the words, "Thy will be done," but upon arising makes no effort to "seek first His kingdom." Instead, the themes of fame, fashion, and fortune are repeated each week as in a television sitcom.

Tuned in are our children, who observe that our actions point to our motivations. Dick Keyes warns parents of the need for right living: "Our lives need to be attractive to our children in the ways that matter most. These ways do not involve our possessions or our professions as much as they do our allegiances. If we have ultimate allegiance to Christ, we will be far from perfect, but we will have integrity before them."[22]

Belonging to Others

I have been blessed by the example of my parents. Our first term on the mission field was cut short due to severe medical problems—my father's tuberculosis and my mother's need for a spinal fusion. My father continued his medical training at Memorial Sloan-Kettering Cancer Center in New York City where he served as the Chief Surgery Resident. His reputation as a physician at this nationally recognized cancer research center was on a meteoric rise. He was offered a position at a salary many times his missionary stipend to join Memorial Sloan-Kettering after residency. But he refused, for he knew his calling was elsewhere.

Years later he would write, "Some have ministered to the untouchables, others to the proud; some to the disgraced, others to the ungrateful. My parish is an assembly of cancer victims in southwest Korea. This is my flock; this is my garden of trampled flowers and bruised reeds. . . . From them I have learned the dimensions of courage and the cost of faith."[23] What my father learned from watching his patients, his son learned from watching his father.

But the story goes back even further. My father's parents were also Presbyterian missionaries; they served in Chile and then in Colombia. It was from them that my father learned his strong sense of calling, and that he should seek to make the world a better place. On my grandmother's wall in Colombia were these words: "No man is great unless he is servant of a cause greater than himself." The scriptural basis is Mark 10:45: "For even the Son of Man did not come to be served, but to serve, and to give his life as a ransom for many."

For two generations now I have witnessed lives lived for others — lives for whom serving the kingdom of God is the highest allegiance. And it must be said that a sense of calling or vocation is not limited to missionaries and ministers. God's call is simply the answer of a life under His authority. It is living in our individual circumstances in union with Jesus, so that through our personalities, talents, and interests the spirit and structures of evil around us are overcome with truth, freedom, and love. My parents are far from perfect, but their obedience to their calling is undeniable. They can say with Paul, "We were not disobedient to our heavenly vision."[24]

FAITHFULNESS UNDER FIRE

Perhaps the most important lesson for children comes when their parents are under fire through failure, illness, or other crises. Suffering tests one's mettle and reveals our character. But many parents make the mistake of shielding their children — particularly adolescents — from the inevitable stresses that come with life.

I faced such a crisis a number of years ago when the leader of an organization I worked for asked me, in effect, to lie in a public document over which I had personal responsibility. I made my protest through the usual channels, but it fell on deaf ears. The institution's public face was deemed more important than its private integrity. After counsel from godly and trusted friends,

I wrote a public statement of protest. Knowing that I might lose my position within days, I called my children together and explained the situation. "Whistleblowers," I said, "are never popular. But before the Lord I feel compelled to speak up." On our knees as a family, we faced the challenge together.

But it is not just in the big events of our lives that we set our example; it's in the everyday occurrences. It's how we respond to the police officer who has just pulled us over for speeding when the car is filled with our teenagers. It's how we act when it is more convenient and less costly to fudge the truth. Integrity is not learned if it is not witnessed.

I have always sought to take one of my children with me when traveling to give a speech. When Alex was thirteen, he accompanied me to a speaking engagement on the impact of electronic entertainment on the moral development of children. The talk touched on video games, MTV, and the Internet, all subjects in which Alex was a self-styled expert.

Our drive home was in a Northeaster — a driving rain that flooded roads, closed bridges, and stopped ferries. As our vehicle was a Land Rover, we felt mildly invincible and pitied the stranded motorist and abandoned cars that littered the highway. Needing gas, I entered an area of New York City that didn't look terribly safe. When pulling out of the gas station, I backed up and collided with an unseen car. The driver was a lost German tourist who was limited in his English and desperate to make a flight at Kennedy Airport.

From the commotion that ensued, one would have thought we had collided head-on. I pointed out that only his rental car's license plate was bent, but he demanded that we call the police. I tried to explain that New York's finest were occupied with far more pressing matters due to the storm. As if to emphasize my point, fire trucks raced by with lights blazing and sirens screeching. Finally, I gave him all the cash I had on me — thirty dollars I recall — and left feeling vaguely relieved that the problem was solved.

Back on the highway, barely able to see the road markers for the rain, I suddenly realized I had no money for the Throgs Neck Bridge, which loomed ahead. There was no way to turn around. Alex moaned, "Dad, you're always getting into trouble." What would I do as I approached the tollgate short the needed three dollars? Would I speed on through? Lie to the toll operator?

It was a moment of decision and Alex was watching my every move. I had no idea what would happen, but at the tollbooth I told the truth about my accident with a German tourist to whom I had given all my money. The police were summoned and I was given a three-dollar bill to pay upon arriving at home. The ethics class that had just transpired was worth far more.

We're not always so levelheaded. Too often we lose it and fly off the handle in anger, defensiveness, or worse. Sometimes we don't tell the truth in front of our children. Then, if our integrity is to be earned, restitution and forgiveness have to be sought.

More than anyone else, our lives are lived before our children. The choices we make in private and public are the lessons they learn about how life is to be negotiated. If we don't let them enter into our stresses and struggles, they will have to find the answers from the fictional adults on television or film or from the parents of their peers. We do well to weigh in while they are still watching.

What story does our life tell? In what are we investing? Is our legacy something for which our children will be proud? Do they see that our words match our actions? Our influence begins with the purpose and integrity of our lives. But it will be distant and disconnected unless we make a conscious effort to connect with our teenage children and their world.

CHAPTER TWELVE

Going Native

PRIORITY:
Be Students of Our Teenager's World

REQUIREMENTS OF FOLLOWERSHIP

By the command of his teacher, Johnny was made to sit. But while doing so he announced to the class resolutely, "I may be sitting, but I'm standing up inside." Johnny shows that people live from their hearts, and that real influence works through another's will, not against it. True leadership is the art of followership.

This is the thesis of historian Garry Wills in his important book on leadership, *Certain Trumpets: The Call of Leaders*. "The leader," Wills explains, "needs to understand followers far more than they need to understand him. . . . There is something selfless in the very selfishness of leaders—they must see things as the followers see them in order to recruit those followers."[1] Followers do not submit to a leader, but join him or her in a shared goal.

The leaders we follow reflect the motivations of our hearts. Wills says, "Show me your leader, and you have bared your soul."[2] Parents may want to pretend that children should automatically follow their commands. But the true challenge is not outward compliance or defiance; it is influencing at the level of the heart. Anyone can give orders, but who will come when we call? And if they do, will it be willingly? "Authentic leaders," Parker Palmer reminds us, "in every setting—from families to nation states—aim at liberating the heart, their own and others', so that its powers can liberate the world."[3]

Pointing back to what we discussed in the previous two chapters, parental leadership starts with the life story embodied by us as parents. Howard Gardner, Harvard professor of education, writes,

> The ultimate impact of the leader depends most significantly on the particular story that he or she relates or embodies, and the receptions to that story on the part of audiences. . . . Effectiveness here involves fit—the story needs to make sense to audience members at this particular historical moment, in terms of where they have been and where they would like to go."[4]

Parental leadership requires that parents become students of their teenager's world, for to lead we must first become a student of those we seek to influence. Dallas Willard suggests that we must study what our children *actually* believe in contrast to what they *profess* to believe. He writes, "What has to be done, instead of trying to drive people to do what we think they are suppose to do, is to be honest about what we and others really believe."[5] What is obvious within the world of corporate, political, and military leadership is too often a forgotten premise of effective parenting.

A TOTALLY ALIEN LIFE-FORM

Too frequently parents today are confused by and afraid of their teenagers. They often adopt an approach of holding their breath, turning their eyes, and stopping up their ears until the hurricane of hormones is past. "People look at teenagers like we're a totally alien life-form," says one eighteen-year-old.[6]

Kids may checkout from family life, but this does not excuse us from disengaging from their life. We need to become anthropologists of adolescent culture—we need to approach the teen world with real interest, not with preconceived judgment. The goal is not to heighten our surveillance or perfect our condemnation, but simply to understand how the world looks from their perspective. Understanding then provides the bridge to communication and friendship.

The goal is not to be a teen—parents who are too "hip-by-half." Nor do we have to like or even appreciate our teenager's selection of music or dress. We should, however, ask how these choices function within our child's developing adolescent identity. What do we learn about our teenager's heart by the friends he or she makes?

Our goal is to be adults who have a mature understanding of the complex world in which our teenager is living. We should seek to feel in some small way what it is like to be a teen today. Once parents can empathize, they can begin to influence. As Paul Tripp, author of *Age of Opportunity: A Biblical Guide to Parenting Teens*, wisely counsels: "Enter the world of your teenager and stay there. Don't ever let them view you as being outside their functional world. Teenagers will reject grenades of wisdom and correction lobbed from afar by someone who has not been on site for quite awhile."[7]

LEARNING THE BIG PICTURE

The first step, then, is to stop talking and to start listening. By and large, we parents do not listen to our kids, for we are too busy telling them how to think and what to do. Moreover, if we have already decided that we don't like teenagers, then why bother with them? Fathers are particularly guilty of this attitude—at precisely the moment their influence is needed most.

Parental followership is time-consuming. It means moving out of one's comfort zone and entering into the world of one's child. Equally important, parental followership requires initially withholding judgment so that we can appreciate the goals, priorities, and patterns of those whom we would influence. Parents must become students of their child's world.

How is this done? The best way is to ask our children to teach us. Of course, this will be met with suspicion if condemnation is the immediately anticipated result. After all, why should our children share something that is an important part of their life if they expect to be put down — "dissed," in youth parlance?

Consequently, a first step may need to be for parents to show a general interest by reading books and articles that examine youth culture. These themselves can be neutral sources for future discussion as we ask our teens whether the perspectives we find match their experiences in school and with their friends. But we have to remember to avoid prying and instead seek general understanding.

Influence begins with refraining from condemnation in relationships; as parents we may need to check our attitude here. "If we would really help those close to us and dear, and if we would learn to live together with our family and 'neighbors' in the power of the kingdom, we must abandon the deeply rooted human practice of condemning and blaming," writes Dallas Willard.[8]

Reading this book is a good beginning. You will certainly know a lot more than most Christian parents of teenagers. If you want to learn even more, then you might start with three books that provide an overview of youth culture from within the perspectives of young people themselves. While I don't always agree with the authors' interpretive conclusions, together the books are uniquely insightful into the world of our teenagers.

Patricia Hersch, *A Tribe Apart: A Journey into the Heart of American Adolescence* (New York: Fawcett Columbine, 1998). ISBN 0-449-90767-8.

Patricia Hersch is a former contributing editor to *Psychology Today* and a journalist who has written for numerous newspapers and magazines. Her book traces the lives of eight regular kids ranging from the seventh to the twelfth grades in Reston, Virginia, a suburban community located outside of Washington, D.C. The power of *A Tribe Apart* is its focus on "mainstream" teens, those who "appear balanced, willing to work, relatively well-behaved, and respectful."[9] Hersch follows these kids over the course of three years, listening to their stories and traumas as they mature into young adults. What unfolds is a gripping, sobering, and heartrending story of what teenage life is like within the average American suburban community.

William Finnegan, *Cold New World: Growing Up in a Harder Country* (New York: Random House, 1998). ISBN 0-679-44870-5.

William Finnegan is a staff writer for the *New Yorker* and an award-winning author. His book takes more of a class argument than Hersch's largely psychological portrait of youth. His is the story of "postmodern poverty," the lives of working-class youth. He spent time with four families in four communities: New Haven, Connecticut; San Augustine County, Texas; the Yakima Valley in Washington State; and the Antelope Valley in northern Los Angeles County. His book reveals a subculture where inequality and cultural alienation are rampant.

Cristina Rathbone, *On the Outside Looking In: A Year in an Inner-City High School* (New York: Atlantic Monthly Press, 1998). ISBN 0-87113-707-0.

Cristina Rathbone grew up in England but attended New York University, and her journalist perspective has a Tocquevillesque feel of an outsider looking in. In telling the story of New York City's West Side High School she provides a sensitive portrayal of urban youth. After a year, Rathbone writes, "I hadn't met one kid at West Side who was disposable. Even the most antisocial of the students I'd come to know during my year were not, finally, so different from me. Some of them were confused and angry, but given the same circumstances, I was convinced that I would have turned out just like them. It was the difference in where we were born, and to whom, that separated us—not the difference in who we were."[10] As hip-hop, urban street perspectives are becoming mainstream, this book deserves a wider reading than by only those concerned with urban youth.

Second in becoming a student of our teen's world is to consider reading youth-oriented magazines such as *Rolling Stone, Spin,* and *Details.* Through the advertisements as much as the feature articles will we be initiated into the language, music, and fashion of youth culture. Much will be highly offensive to adult, not to speak of Christian, sensibilities. For these are the tabloids of the deathwork culture—the commodified myths of rebellion sold to youthful consumers by adult-run corporations.

Third, listen to pop music on a variety of radio formats as well as television video channels, such as MTV and VH-1. Or take a field trip to the local record store to familiarize yourself with the dominant musical genres and the most popular groups. Large record stores allow patrons to listen to music on headphones, so you won't have to buy the CDs. I can't underscore enough the importance music plays in youth culture. You might want to discuss with your teen Bush's album, *The Science of Things* (1999). It features a song, "Jesus Online," which discusses the difficulty of trying to maintain some kind of spiritual awareness in an age of technology.

Fourth, watch teen-oriented TV shows and movies. Here again, we should play the role of cultural critic before we put on the hat of parental police. There is much we can learn from watching episodes of television shows like *Dawson's Creek* or MTV's *Road Rules* with our teen.

Brief assessments of films and music are available from Christian bookstores and the Internet, but I discourage such shortcuts. Not only do they hinder us from understanding our teen's world for ourselves, but they are usually aimed at strengthening parental control. Moreover, I have found that kids will listen to our perspective on a film or CD if we have taken it seriously without being flippantly dismissive.

Many films, videos, and CDs may prove offensive to Christian parents. But we must have some personal exposure in order to speak intelligently to our children. Teen film director Chris Weitz explains, "High school *isn't* PG-13."[11] Consequently, any honest assessment of youth culture inevitably is going to push the boundaries of mature taste and propriety. Parents may choose to play the ostrich, but our children do not have that luxury.

Understanding demands some honest exposure, however uncomfortable we might feel. At times we will be deeply moved. For instance, I cannot listen to Sarah McLachlan's "Dear God"[12] or the Indigo Girls' "Closer to Fine"[13] without shedding tears. It is these tears that give us the connection to our teens, establishing the context for influence.

SHEEPDOGS OR SHEPHERDS?

As parents we are to love and lead our children as God loves and leads us. Just as we are shepherded by Jesus, so too we are to shepherd our flock. How do shepherds lead? Answering this question provides the foundation to parenting.

Jesus explains, "The man who enters by the gate is the shepherd of his sheep. The watchman opens the gate for him, and the sheep listen to his voice. He calls his own sheep by name and leads them out. When he has brought out all his own, he goes on ahead of them, and his sheep follow him because they know his voice" (John 10:2-4). In this short parable resides the key to our influence as parents.

First, Jesus enters through a guarded gate, which is the door to our relationship to Him. "I am the gate," He says, emphasizing that He is the way of access to life as God intended. The sheepfolds of our hearts should be always guarded—for here resides the core of who we are, the source of our feelings, reason, and will. But Jesus, we note, enters the sheepfold without creating alarm. There is no defensiveness as He approaches and for Him the gate is opened because "the sheep know his voice." This is not a voice of condemnation or abuse, but that of the one who "lays down his life for the sheep" (John 10:11).

In contrast, the hired shepherd has no personal interest or investment in the sheep and abandons them at the first sign of crisis. Not so with the true shepherd; He will defend the sheep even until death.

And so the shepherd leads simply by walking ahead of the flock with the sheep following willingly. Dallas Willard observes, "To manipulate and manage people—to drive them—is not the same thing as to *lead* them. The sheepdog nips and harasses the sheep, while the shepherd simply calls as he calmly walks ahead of the sheep."[14] The sheep follow because they know the character of the shepherd.

Peter later reflected on Jesus' words: "Be shepherds of God's flock that is under your care, serving as overseers—not because you must, but because you are willing, as God wants you to be; not greedy for money, but eager to serve; not lording it over those entrusted to you, but being examples to the flock" (1 Peter 5:2-3).

True leadership is self-giving service for the good of others. And so is true parenting. It is achieved not by coercion, but by the power of example.

Our influence with our children is based on whether they know our voice to be one of love and not condemnation. Only then will they follow our example as we walk before them. Dallas Willard concludes, "The outcome is really the work of the guided individuals, not merely of the one who is guiding. These individuals' uniqueness counts before God and must not be over-ridden. It remains their life, after all, because we have 'guided' them only through their own understanding, deliberation, and decision."[15]

If our children are to know that we are for them, we must make every effort to understand their world—including the hired hands and the wolves who surround them. Only then will they know our voice and open the gate when we approach their hearts. An important aspect of establishing a connection with our child is to become an advocate for their constructive interests.

CHAPTER THIRTEEN

"Proud Parent of a Skateboarder"

PRIORITY:
*Become an Advocate of Our Child's
Constructive Interests*

IN MY FATHER'S EYES

A father taking his son hunting for the first time is an American rite-of-passage. Of course, it doesn't have to be hunting—it could be football, basketball, sailing, or car racing, as well as visiting an art gallery, library, or orchestra performance. The likes and dislikes of a father often come to define manhood for sons just as the likes and dislikes of a mother often define womanhood for daughters. It is a pattern with an ancient and troubled pedigree. Consider the tensions of the father-son relationship in Nicholas Evans's novel, *The Loop*.

Thirteen-year-old Luke was now Buck Calder's only son, as his brother Henry had been killed in a tragic car accident six years before. Luke and Henry had been as different as Esau and Jacob—Luke with his sensitive nature took after his mother, and Henry with his rugged toughness took after his father.

And now Luke's father had asked him if he wanted to try for his first elk. Luke had been dreading the invitation and yet was hurt that it was so long in coming. They went off to a hidden canyon, barely speaking as they crunched through the snow. Luke could hear the thumping of his heart and prayed crazily that the elk would fight and save themselves.

The elk hadn't heard his heartbeat. Across the canyon, there was a herd of maybe twenty cows. A little way off, a solitary bull with five-point antlers was nibbling bark. . . . Luke handed the binoculars back to his father and wondered if he dared say that he didn't want to go through with it. But he knew that even if he were to try, the words would never come out; their effect would be too catastrophic. . . .

The intimacy of the scope was shocking. Luke could make out individual hairs on the dark neck. He could see the grinding of the jaws as the elk chewed, see the paler patches around the liquid black eyes that impassively surveyed the cows, see droplets of melted snow on his nose. . . .

Half of Luke's brain screamed at him to hand his father the gun right then. But the other half assessed this moment for what it was: a final chance to *be* something in his father's eyes. He must take this creature's life for his own to have any value.[1]

That day was a defining moment for the relationship between Luke and Buck Calder. Luke realized that he was not free to be himself and still be appreciated by his father. In using this example, I must underline that I have nothing against hunting, and in fact, love alpine mountaineering and off-road driving. Nor is the need for approval and understanding limited only to fathers and sons. There are just as many mothers who, say, dream of their daughters being selected homecoming queen while their daughters would rather "haul butt" in the back bowl on their snowboard.

The point of the excerpt is to illustrate that our children are not an extension of our own identity. Singer Alanis Morissette presses this point home in her song, "Perfect":

I'll live through you
I'll make you what I never was
If you're the best, then maybe so am I
Compared to him compared to her
I'm doing this for your own damn good
You'll make up for what I blew
What's the problem . . . why are you crying[2]

Tori Amos sings of a sixteen-year-old, "She's been everybody else's girl, maybe one day she'll be her own."[3] Teenagers are crying out to be their own persons. As parents we are responsible to affirm their unique and distinctive individuality—however different they may be in temperament and interests from us or from their siblings. In practical terms, we must become advocates for our teenager's constructive interests.

A SENSE OF FIT

We need to become students not only of our teenagers' world but also of their own unique perceptions on their world. We should learn something about their favorite authors, artists, and musical groups. We should seek to understand their passions, whether the environment or the plight of political prisoners. Spiritually speaking, parents should encourage their children to explore a wide variety of experiences that will set the backdrop for discovering their life's work.

The Puritans get a bad rap today as being dour, judgmental prudes, but they have a great deal to say to us on this matter of lifework. Theologian J. I. Packer observes that while we are spiritual dwarfs, they were giants. They "were great souls serving a great God. In them clear-headed passion and warm-hearted compassion combined."[4]

The patriarch of English Puritanism was William Perkins (1558-1602). Shortly before his death he wrote "A Treatise of the Vocations or Callings of Men," in which he sought to help his parishioners think broadly about the most basic purpose of their lives. He was instructing them not only to follow Jesus generally, but to carry out their obedience to Christ in a way that was unique to their individual character. Perkins sets the adolescent question "What do I want to be when I grow up?" within this larger conception of calling. He gives us five rules to consider as we think about our own particular calling and that of our teens— the unique place and way we express Christ's lordship in our lives.

1. Without exception, every person of every degree, state, sex, or condition must have some personal and particular calling.

2. Every person must judge that particular calling in which God has placed him to be the best of all callings for him: I say not simply best, but best for him.
3. Every person must join the practice of his personal calling with the practices of the general calling of Christianity.
4. Those who bear public callings must first reform themselves in private.
5. A particular calling must give place to the general calling of a Christian when they cannot both stand together.[5]

At the heart of Perkins' understanding of personal calling is the idea of "fit": "Everyone must choose a fit calling to walk in, that is, every calling must be fitted to the person and every person fitted to the calling." This process involves some trial and error and ideally will include wise counsel from those who know us well and are themselves spiritually mature. "Men of years make choice of fit callings for themselves when they try, judge, and examine themselves as to what things they are apt and fit, and to what things they are not," Perkins advises. "Fit" includes both what a person most desires as well as the ability to accomplish it.

Parents play an important role in helping their children examine their inclinations and aptitudes in light of their life as a calling before the Lord. "It is the duty of parents to make choice of fit calling for them, before they apply them to any particular condition of life," Perkins explains. "And the truth is that parents cannot do greater wrong to their children and the society of men than to apply them to unfit callings."

Obviously, today parents have far less say and children have a much wider range of career choices than in Perkins' day. But the spiritual principles remain. Frederick Buechner argues that our life's work will be found in the intersection of our deepest gladness and the world's greatest need.

There are all different kinds of voices calling you to all different kinds of work, and the problem is to find out which is the voice of God rather than of society, say, or the super-ego, or self-interest. By and large a good rule for finding out is this: the kind of work God usually calls you to is the kind of work (a) that you need most to do and (b) the world most needs to have done. If you really get a kick out of your work, you've presumably met requirement (a), but if your work is writing TV deodorant commercials, the chances are you've missed requirement (b). On the other hand, if your work is being a doctor in a leper colony, you have probably met (b), but if most of the time you're bored or depressed by it, the chances are you haven't only by-passed (a) but probably aren't helping your patients much either. Neither the hair shirt nor the soft berth will do. The place God calls you to is the place where your deep glad-ness and the world's deep hunger meet.[6]

As parents we must first understand our own lives as a response to God's summons before we help our children see their lives in this light.[7] As we do so, we have a responsibility to allow our children to explore a wide variety of ways in which they could serve the common good. We don't need a Ph.D. in child psy-chology to appreciate the unique direction, interests, and abilities of our children. When our children hit the teenage years, they need the space and freedom to let these develop.

As parents we need to listen to our children's dreams and aspirations. At age eighteen C. S. Lewis knew as he took his Oxford scholarship exams that "there was hardly any position in the world save that of a don in which I was fitted to earn a living, and that I was staking everything on a game in which few won and hundreds lost."[8] Yet his every attempt to discuss his dream with his father was met with failure: "His intense desire for my total confidence coexisted with an inability to listen (in any strict sense) to what I said. He could never empty, or silence, his own mind to make room for an alien thought."[9] Similarly, many par-ents quench the fire that fuels their children's dreams.

OF GRINDS AND HALF-PIPES

Adolescence is a time of growing independence. While this desire must be managed, parents also must be in favor of it. Dick Keyes warns, "A prepackaged agenda for a child's life is either a pre-scription for crushed and resentful obedience or an invitation to outright rebellion."[10] For instance, I studiously avoided becoming a surgeon—named as I am for my father—though I did later become a wilderness emergency medical technician.

Likewise, my boys avoided following in my footsteps athlet-ically; instead, David took up lacrosse and Alex skateboarding. Also, both became active in theater—David as a lighting tech-nician and Alex as an actor. This was a long way from anything I ever did in high school. I don't believe it was a conscious choice on their part, but both boys moved into worlds in which they were the experts, not me. I couldn't cradle a lax ball or ollie a curb, but I still had a vital role to play in understanding and encouraging their pursuits.

For my youngest son, Alex, I thought skateboarding was a pass-ing fad—like, say, baseball cards were in elementary school. But the board-sports lifestyle of skateboarding, snowboarding, and surfing has become Alex's passion. He announced one day that he would not play any sports where coaches yelled. Football—my adolescent dream—was out. I simply needed to accept this as Alex's way.

If this was his deal, then I wanted to be totally behind it. So off we went to the summer Extreme Games held in Newport, Rhode Island, where I was given a crash course in the adrenaline-rush of alternative sports—sky surfing, bungy jumping, BMX biking, inline skating, skateboarding, street luge, and sport climbing.

The day before the event, Alex insisted on doing reconnais-sance for the best seats. They turned out to be directly behind the official photographers and weren't actually seats—it was standing-room only. So the next morning, two hours before the gates opened, we were there with our X-Games hats and me loaded down with camera-gear, looking the part of the official sports photographer.

I was immersed in Alex's world—the skater aficionados whose conversation of grinds, ollies, rail-slides, and 360-kick flips mixed in with the booming Ska music. I found myself cheering until hoarse, fighting wildly for skateboards thrown into the crowd, and altogether having one of the most memorable times I've ever spent with my son. Alex and I connected—on his terms, in his world.

I'm not naïve to the reputation or injuries of those involved in board sports. More than once, my ambulance crew has been called out to assist an injured skater who tried to rail slide down a twenty-foot staircase or ollie a concrete canyon. Skateboarders are widely viewed as the urban outlaws of parking lots and school playgrounds. But mostly, skaters—and the entire alternative sports world—are simply part of a culture parents have not taken the time to understand or appreciate. I've often thought of having a bumper sticker printed that states, "Proud Parent of a Skateboarder."

TRUE CONNECTION

Your teenager may have more "normal" passions—horses, books, ballet, perhaps even football. Rather than just leaving our children to their peers, we need to find ways of supporting and encouraging their constructive interests. William Perkins never dreamed of the Extreme Games when he wrote his advice to parents in 1600. But through these experiences Alex was learning his "fit."

Inspired by the X-Game photos, Alex began to take up an interest in photography and has shown an amazing "photographic eye." Over my desk hangs a beautiful picture he took in Ireland of a Celtic cross bathed in a lush, green fog. Its subdued shades are a long way from the vert ramps and street parks of the skateboard competition that summer day in Newport. But it was there, watching his father take pictures of his heroes, that the genesis of Alex's photographic interest was born.

The other day, I received the following e-mail from Alex, a ninth-grader attending a boarding school in New York.

> Dad,
>
> I called last night and there was no answer, but I will call again today. Saturday night Tim, John, and I set up a kicker ramp in the gym. It was so much fun. I did this one ollie that almost cleared Tim's head!! (and you know how big Tim is). I was also landing 360 flips!! Not off the ramp, just on the flat ground, but it was still pretty exciting. My wrist still aches, but it is all right.

Sunday, we had our third SBFL football game. We were playing the first place team. If you don't remember, our team is made up of almost all soccer players. Our QB is Mr. Hogan and has only played Australian football. Well, anyway, the game went back and forth for a while until the second half. There were two minutes left in the game (we were up by two) fourth down and the other team had the ball on our ten-yard line. Shep and I were covering Bobby Balister who is incredibly fast. Mr. Hunt threw a high loft to Bobby, Shep and I both dove for it collided in mid-air and some how blocked the ball. I'm not sure which one of us blocked it, but, whatever, it was amazing.

We then continued from our ten to drive down the field to their fifteen-yard line. Once again it was fourth down, but we had the ball. We needed about ten to get the first down and keep the clock going. All I did was a simple post pattern and beat my defender. All I remember was jumping up for the ball and waking up on the one-yard line with Mark Simmons and the rest of my teammates huddled around me screaming that I had won the game for us. With about ten seconds left we just ran out the clock. It was really intense and I am extremely sore. I think I did the same thing again to my shoulder, but at least we won. It was worth the pain to see the look on those football play-ers' faces when they realized they got beat by a bunch of soccer players and skaters.

Love,

Your extremely sore but happy Alex!!!

What does it take to get a note like this from your fifteen-year-old son? Connecting—on his terms. The proud parent of a skateboarder, indeed.

CHAPTER FOURTEEN

Reality Bites

PRIORITY:
*Establish Limits Based on the Objective
Truth of Reality*

"QUESTION AUTHORITY"

We can learn a lot through a quick perusal of a high-school parking lot. Here we find evidence of the adolescence truism that "advertising is existence." Plastered on the back of every car, van, and pickup are the tribal markers of youth culture, such as "You can send me to college, but you can't make me think," or the old standby, "Question Authority." Teens live in a world where the question-begging slogan "Just Say No" is the purported answer to an expanding list of social behaviors. The motto's rhetorical appeal and moral authority are empty. No wonder teenagers question authority.

The priority of parental influence, then, is this: Before we establish specific moral guidelines for our teenagers, we need to establish whether what we are putting into place is a personal choice, communal covenant, or objective law. The sixteen-year-old's question, "Why?" is not impertinent. Why abstinence and not free sex? Why truth-telling and not lies? Why respect for property and not stealing? What makes some behaviors right and others wrong? How do parents know, anyway? Why should teenagers listen to parents and follow their moral guidelines?

What is the basis of parental authority? While the questions may seem abstract, in the answers lies the moral foundation upon which parental authority rests.

THREE TYPES OF AUTHORITY

Sociologist Max Weber suggests three different types of social authority. Although they may overlap somewhat, his threefold distinction provides some helpful observations.[1]

1. Personal Authority

The first type Weber describes as "charismatic authority," or what I call *personal authority*. Here authority is based on one's perceived saintliness, heroism, or exemplary character. One's followers are loyal to those characteristics that make the leader special.

Many children, and particularly young children, follow their parents' admonitions simply because of their innate trust in their parents. They assume the authority of their father and mother as a matter of course—"He's my Dad," and "She's my Mom." When such authority is challenged, however, the dissent frequently becomes an attack on the person: "You don't love me," or, "You're no better than me." Likewise, the parents' response to such a challenge is frequently emotional: "Look at all the sacrifices I've made for you over the years," or, "I'm older and wiser." Guilt or an entreaty to one's personal status or character is used to keep the child's loyalty. When challenges persist, the appeal often shifts to the second type of authority.

2. Positional Authority

Weber calls his second type "legal authority," or what I describe as *positional authority*. Here authority is based on an institutional position and the rules and regulations that go with it. In this type of authority, the personal characteristics of the authority figure do not matter as much as the impersonal role or office they hold. Authority is based on the position, not the person; the institution, not the individual.

Parents everywhere have appealed to positional authority at some time or other. In conflict with a child, the mother might respond, "I'm the parent and that's that!" Or the father might say, "When you're the parent, you can do it your way." The appeal here is not based on the fact that the parent is loving or wise, but simply the parent. When the challenge to authority persists, the use of coercive sanctions are often necessary to maintain respect for the position of authority.

This is the authority of teachers and police—impersonal, bureaucratic, and rule-based. It doesn't matter if the police officer smiles or the teacher is kind; their authority resides in their position. But deference to this type of authority has weakened among teens. The divorce of parents, the sexual misconduct of teachers, and the brutality of police have undermined positional respect.

3. Principled Authority

The final type of authority Weber calls "traditional authority," or what I call *principled authority*. Here authority is based on fidelity to long-established principles and powers that do not depend on one's personal characteristics or positional role. The focus here is on the content of the obligations and the mutual responsibility of both the authority figure and the followers to be submissive to these shared principles.

When a child challenges such authority, parents don't have to be defensive about their relationship with their child nor coercive in demanding respect. Instead, they simply remind the child of the mutual obligations that bind them both: "Son, we live in the kind of world where such choices lead to painful consequences." Wisdom stems from the lessons of reality. The parents' role is to teach the objectivity of moral principles under whose authority both parent and child stand.

This third type of parental authority needs to be restored in our day. Understood in this light, the impeachment crisis of the Clinton presidency was a disagreement between those who saw his failings as undermining his personal but not his positional authority and those who saw his actions as an abuse of principled authority. In the end, the therapeutic and procedural triumphed over the moral. But it must not be so within our homes.

REJECTING REALITY

Remember the adolescent bumper sticker, "Question Authority"? We can now add to the other fender one that proclaims, "Question Reality." This is the heart of our challenge as parents today. Ours is not the first time parental authority has been challenged, but ours is the first time that the popular understanding of truth and morality has been conceptually removed from any correspondence to objective reality. Ours is the first civilization to abandon objective morality in theory, not just in practice.

I began to see this when I taught Bible to high-school seniors at a college prep school. My classes were filled with students from a variety of religious traditions: Jews, Muslims, Buddhists, Christians, and the omnipresent adolescent agnostic. Although the class was a requirement for graduation, it did not show up on the student's college transcript. Consequently, it was frequently met with more than its share of senior disinterest.

After teaching the class a number of times, I realized that the students could memorize the Bible verses, ace the exams, and never understand the objective truth of the gospel. They automatically assumed that any discussion of Christianity was a consideration of a subjective reality—merely one opinion in the midst of many. I thought I was teaching truth, but they were hearing opinions. Using the very same words, we were talking about two distinct realities.

Although an agnostic, Somerset Maugham acknowledged, "In religion above all things the only thing of use is an objective truth. The only God that is of use is a being who is personal, supreme, and good, and whose existence is as certain as that two and two make four."[2] Such a view of God was a foreign concept to my students—and will be for most teenagers.

As we have seen, the essence of the deathwork culture is the progressive escape from the requirements of *lived* reality to the unconstraint of *assumed* reality. Sociologist James Nolan observes, "Therapeutic language allows us to understand ourselves through self-creation rather than through the pursuit of truth. . . . As such, one's understanding of oneself is not limited by references to things outside of the self."[3]

When there are no objective standards of moral behavior, sub-jective desires reign supreme. And when feelings rule the will, the mind is powerless and our animal natures will run amuck. In the midst of World War II, C. S. Lewis became aware of school text-books that taught what is now common in schools across the nation—the belief that moral values are subjective. Such views, he wrote, silence any criticism of the Holocaust:

> Everyone is indignant when he hears the Germans define justice as that which is in the interest of the Third Reich. But it is not always remembered that this indignation is per-fectly groundless if we ourselves regard morality as subjective sentiment to be altered at will. Unless there is some objective standard of good, over-arching Germans, Japanese, and ourselves alike whether any of us obey it or not, then of course the Germans are as competent to create their ideology as we are to create ours. . . . Unless the measuring rod is independent of the thing measured, we can do no measuring.[4]

As Lewis scholar Michael Aeschliman explains, "The tri-umph of personal desire over objective validity as a standard of behavior creates what is tantamount to a moral vacuum into which will rush disordered passions bloated in their abnormal freedom from any constraint."[5]

The seductiveness of unconstrained reality is the promise of cyberspace. At its most extreme, Los Angeles-based Extropians advocate the futuristic possibility of "downloading" the mind into a virtual world. It is the premise of the sci-fi film, "The Lawnmower Man" (1992). Cultural critic Mark Dery explains that such extropian transhumanism is a marriage of Ayn Rand and Friedrich Nietzsche—a combination of Rand's libertarianism and Nietzsche's morality.[6] It's a scary thought. Here the constraints of the physical body are abandoned for an unconstrained cyber-consciousness. Dery calls this "the theology of the ejector seat."

Science fiction nonsense? Perhaps. But such views are on a continuum of increasing disconnectedness from reality—first morality, then science, finally humanity itself. Or as David

Cronenberg's sci-fi film, *Videodrome* (1982), puts it, "First you see video. Then you wear video. Then you eat video. Then you *be* video."[7] This is far-out stuff. But it is important to realize that these are increasingly common assumptions of the deathwork culture in which our children live.

DENYING THE UNDENIABLE

In light of the deathwork culture, a vigorous defense of the objective nature of morality must precede any parental list of behavioral expectations. Our desire is not simply that our teens will conform to our household guidelines. Rather, we should enable them to learn something about the laws of human nature, about how God designed them to live within an objective creation. Before we apply the rod of discipline, we must confirm the existence of a measuring rod.

We must affirm in both practice and theory the givenness of traditional morality, which is not unique to Christianity but common to humanity. Traditional notions of right and wrong are found in Chinese, Sanskrit, Babylonian, Roman, Greek, Native American, and aboriginal philosophies and religions.

The view that ethical norms vary widely between civilizations and cultures is a figment of modern imagination not based in scholarship. For instance, anthropologist Margaret Mead's portrayal of Samoa, a paradise of free love and casual sex as depicted in such films as *Blue Lagoon* (1980), was based on an academic fraud. It was later shown that the Samoans were fierce defenders of female chastity and regarded both premarital sex and adultery with horror.[8]

"The idea that Christianity brought a new ethical code into the world is a grave error," writes C. S. Lewis. "Only serious ignorance of Jewish and Pagan culture would lead anyone to the conclusion that it is a radically new thing. . . . In triumphant monotony the same indispensable platitudes will meet us in culture after culture."[9]

Moreover, Lewis argues that traditional morality is so basic *to* life that it is a premise *of* life. Human morality doesn't start from a blank slate that is subsequently informed by experience, argued to by reason, or constructed by culture. Such is the combined

hubris of rationalism and subjectivism. Traditional morality is neither discovered nor invented; it is simply known. Our problem isn't
ignorance, but iniquity. It isn't *knowing* morality, but *being* moral.

We do have a moral choice. Contrary to popular opinion, however, it is not that of picking and choosing our morality. Rather it is
the choice between traditional morality or no morality at all. There
is no halfway morality. "The Nietzschean ethic can be accepted only
if we are ready to scrap traditional morals as a mere error and then
to put ourselves in a position where we find no ground for any value
judgements at all," Lewis writes in *The Abolition of Man*.[10]

And yet we all know the proclivity toward picking and choosing morality—a little more for you, a little less for me. "The fear
of permanent, objective moral laws is amazingly selective,"
writes Peter Kreeft. "It almost always comes down to just one area:
sex."[11] Few are as honest as Augustine's adolescent prayer, "Grant
me chastity and continence, but *not yet*."[12]

Intellectual rationalization in the service of desire replaces
honest living in the service of truth. This is E. Michael Jones's
argument in his study of modern intellectuals: "In the absence
of virtue, the mind will not stop functioning, it will only stop
functioning in contact with reality. . . . As with syphilis, so
with the moral life: what starts between the legs often ends up
infecting the brain."[13]

Hormones drive more than just the behavior of teens; they
also influence the theories of scholars. "Lust is a common
enough vice, especially in this age. The crucial intellectual event
occurs, however, when vices are transmuted into theories, when
the 'intellectual' sets up shop in rebellion against the moral law
and, therefore, in rebellion against the truth," writes Jones.[14]

As Nietzsche himself acknowledges, "If one would explain
how the abstrusest metaphysical claims of a philosopher really
came about, it is always well (and wise) to ask first: at what
morality does all this (does *he*) aim at?"[15] Nietzsche's suspicion
cuts in both directions. The biographies of leading thinkers go a
long way toward explaining their intellectual rejection of reality
and its requirements.[16] "Almost always, the practice comes
before the theory. . . . Addicts cannot see objective truth clearly,"
explains Peter Kreeft and Ronald Tacelli.[17]

We live in a world filled with this intellectual madness. As George Orwell warned, "We have now sunk to a depth at which re-statement of the obvious is the first duty of intelligent men."[18] Lifelong smokers receive million-dollar court settlements from tobacco companies. We promote mayhem in entertainment and lament violence in schools.[19]

We can no more reject with impunity the requirements of morality than we can the requirements of gravity. The only difference is in the length of time it takes to "hit the deck," as they say in rock climbing. When you step off a cliff the view may be spectacular, the breeze refreshing, and the freedom thrilling, but the adrenaline rush won't last. Neither will it when we step off a moral precipice. "There is a way that seems right to a man, but in the end it leads to death" (Proverbs 14:12).

As Russian novelist Leo Tolstoy warned, "We have created a way of life which is contrary to mankind's moral and physical nature, and yet we want to be free while living this kind of life. Freedom cannot be achieved by looking for it, but in looking for truth. Freedom should not be a purpose, but a consequence."[20]

The only difference between the laws of nature and the laws of human nature is that humans can pretend they don't exist. A person who believes such nonsense is what the Bible calls a "fool." As Lewis says, "If truth is objective, if we live in a world we did not create and cannot change merely by thinking, if the world is not really a dream of our own, then the most destructive belief we could possibly believe would be the denial of this primary fact. It would be closing your eyes while driving, or blissfully ignoring the doctor's warnings."[21] Yet we live in a culture where the blind often lead the blind. The personal wreckage in the lives of young people is a grim testament to the consequences. Theologian David Wells warns, "For in setting off to live and think as we will, we find that we have run headlong into the hard wall of reality, a wall that God himself sustains despite all of our most energetic assaults."[22]

REALITY BITES

The film *Reality Bites* (1994) tells the story of four friends who have just graduated from college. Gone are their carefree days of an educational equivalent to country-club existence. The future remains a haze of unanswered questions and uncertain dreams. And quickly crashing into their lives is the reality of unemployment, the fear of AIDS, the relentless nature of bills, the pain of broken relationships, the loss of meaning. Troy, the slacker artist, intones his nihilistic views: "Life is a random lottery of meaningless tragedy in a series of near escapes. So I take pleasure in the details, like a quarter-pounder with cheese."

As their lives continue to unravel, Elaina, the unemployed college valedictorian, laments, "I just don't understand why things can't go back to normal like on the Brady Bunch or something." Troy retorts caustically, "Because Mr. Brady died of AIDS. Things don't work out that way."

As parents we make a grave mistake when we cushion our children from the requirements of reality. It's true that we need to set age-appropriate limits for our teenage children. But even more important is their understanding that the principles we live by and set for them are grounded in the objective structures of reality. These are not just Dad's whims or Mom's religion. Philosopher Charles Peirce reminds us that "The essence of truth is in its resistance to be ignored."[23] Long before our kids leave home, we need to teach the lesson that *reality bites*.

Experience, it is said, is the best teacher; it surely is the most costly. But more often than not, its lessons are worth its price. Lewis wisely notes, "What I like about experience is that it is such an honest thing. You may take any number of wrong turnings; but keep your eyes open and you will not be allowed to go very far before the signs appear. You may have deceived yourself, but experience is not trying to deceive you. The universe rings true wherever you fairly test it."[24]

I've often been struck by Lewis's daily walk, which he took not for exercise but as a way to stay grounded in a larger and wider world. Agnes Sanford wisely reminds those who struggle with depression — that state of self-constricting introspection — to rest upon the beauty of this world: "The simplest and oldest way in which God manifests Himself is not through people but through and in the earth itself."[25] The objective creation points us to the objective Creator.

We must escape the unreality of the self and live in and toward the real. Pascal wrote, "We are full of things that impel us outwards. Our instinct makes us feel that our happiness must be sought outside ourselves. . . . Thus it is no good philosophers telling us: Withdraw into yourselves and there you will find your good. We do not believe them, and those who do believe them are the most empty and silly of all."[26]

The deepest longings of young people are not for the pseudointimacy of sex or the hyperreality of drugs or the intoxicated happiness of alcohol. These are nothing more than cheap imitations. "We are half-hearted creatures, fooling about with drink and sex and ambition when infinite joy is offered us. . . . We are far too easily pleased."[27] As Lewis continues, "They are not the thing itself; they are only the scent of the flower we have not found, the echo of a tune we have not heard, news from a country we have never yet visited."[28]

Lewis concludes, "What does not satisfy when we find it, was not the thing we were desiring."[29] It is too easy to accept the partial for the whole, the sign for the destination. Yet we long for reality. Leanne Payne states, "The history of fallen man can be summed up as a flight from the radiant substantiveness—the reality of the presence and the face of God."[30]

Helping our teenage children know the difference between the substitute and the Substance is the purpose of the next chapter. Only then will they be able to pray with Augustine, "Give me Thine own self, without which, though Thou shouldst give me all that ever Thou hast made, yet could it not my desires be satisfied."[31]

CHAPTER FIFTEEN

"Whatever"

PRIORITY:
Encourage Passionate Seeking of Truth

DO I BELIEVE?

The time comes when young people take ownership of their own beliefs. This process, which almost always begins during the adolescent years, is important and inevitable. The only question is whether as parents we will have any influence. G. K. Chesterton writes of his own youth, "All I had hitherto heard of Christian theology had alienated me from it. I was a pagan at the age of twelve, and a complete agnostic by the age of sixteen; and I cannot understand any one passing the age of seventeen without having asked himself so simple a question."[1]

As the son of missionaries, I was brought up largely in a closed universe of belief. Almost all of the adults in my life were committed Christians and professional missionaries—ministers, educators, and doctors. Thus when it came time for college, I consciously chose to attend a small liberal arts college that I knew would put my faith to the test. Was Christianity true? Or was it simply the most comfortable route to follow? Over the course of my college years—in a world away from my parents who continued their service in Korea—I set out to take ownership of my beliefs.

My crisis of faith came in the fall of my sophomore year when I was taking a philosophy course in existentialism. We were assigned Miguel de Unamuno's short story, "Saint Emmanuel the Good, Martyr." The story is the memoir of a woman in her fifties who as a young adult had been the deaconess to Don Emmanuel, a Spanish priest. His active service in his village earned him the love of the villagers and the reputation of a saint.

I saw myself in Don Emmanuel: "His life was active rather than contemplative, and he constantly fled from idleness, even from leisure. . . . His constant activity, his ceaseless intervention in the tasks and diversions of everyone, had the appearance, in short, of a flight from himself, of a flight from solitude."[2] But as the story unfolds, we discover that Saint Emmanuel only feigns belief in order to protect the peace, happiness, and illusions of his charges. The aging woman ends her tale with the haunting question: "And I, do I believe?"[3]

For the first time ever, I squarely faced the implications for my life if God did not exist. Unamuno begins his story with this scriptural epigram from Paul: "If only for this life we have hope in Christ, we are to be pitied more than all men" (1 Corinthians 15:19). To this day, I remember the gut-wrenching hollowness in my stomach as I pondered the story. No longer was I a child following in the footsteps of my parents. Instead, I was beginning to make their beliefs my own.

FAMILIARITY BREEDS CONTEMPT

Contemporary young people have been called the "whatever generation," kids who turn affectlessness into a fashion statement and detachment into a lifestyle. "Whatever" is their mantra—sloth as a worldview. Novelist Dorothy Sayers observes that sloth "is the sin which believes in nothing, cares for nothing, seeks to know nothing, interferes with nothing, enjoys nothing, loves nothing, hates nothing, finds purpose in nothing, lives for nothing, and only remains alive because there is nothing it would die for."[4] Far from being unique to young people, sloth has been largely learned from parents. Tom Beaudoin observes, "Many baby boomers had kept institutional religion at arm's length until midlife. For their children, GenXers, the step from religion-as-accessory to religion-as-unnecessary was a slight shuffle, not a long leap."[5]

Nothing is more dangerous than spiritual indifference. Yet nothing is more comfortable. As C. S. Lewis challenges us,

> Floating is a very agreeable operation; a decision either way costs something. Real Christianity and consistent Atheism both make demands on a man. But to admit, on occasion, and as possibilities, all the comforts of one without its discipline— to enjoy all the liberty of the other without its philosophical and emotional abstinences—well, this may be honest, but there's no good pretending it is uncomfortable.[6]

Sloth can be brought on by the all-too-human syndrome of failing to appreciate what is familiar. Whether it is the beauty of our surroundings, the grace of God, or even the girl next door, we frequently take for granted what we know too well. This discontent of familiarity is a common spiritual problem of those who are raised in Christian homes. And it can be compounded when we as parents, when worried about our teenagers, are tempted to increase their exposure to our beliefs. But our desire for our children must not be a conformity to our convictions but their own passionate searching for truth.

Most teens do not lose their faith because they think too much, but because they think too little. They just drift away with an off-putting, "Whatever." Here, quoted at length, is how in 1829 Christian statesman William Wilberforce described this process of drift:

> A typical case of such unbelief begins when young men are brought up as nominal Christians. Their parents take them to church as children and there they become acquainted with those passages of the Bible used in the service. If their parents still keep some of the old habits, they may even be taught the catechism.
>
> But they go off into the world, yield to youthful temptations, neglect to look at their Bible, and they do not develop their religious duties. They do not even try to

reflect, study, or mature in the thoughts that they once might have had as children. They may even travel abroad, relax still further their religious habits, and tend to read only about those controversial issues of religion.

Attending church occasionally, these occasional incidents more often offend such youth than strengthen them. Perhaps they are tempted to be morally superior to those they think are superstitious. Or the poor examples of some professing Christians disgust them. Or else they stumble because of the absurdities of others who see they are equally ignorant to themselves. At any rate, they gradually begin to doubt the reality of Christianity. A confused sense of relief that it is all untrue settles within them.

Impressions deepen, reinforced by fresh arguments. At length they are convinced of their doubts in a broad sweep over the whole realm of religion.

This may not be universally so, but it may be termed the natural history of skepticism. It is the experience of those who have watched the progress of unbelief in those they care about. It is confirmed by the written lines of some of the most eminent unbelievers. We find that they once gave a sort of implicit, inherited assent to the truth of Christianity and were considered believers.

How then did they become skeptics? Reason, thought, and inquiry have little to do with it. Having lived for many years careless and irreligious lives, they eventually matured in their faithlessness—not by force of irreligious strength but by lapse of time. This is generally the offspring of prejudice, and its success is the result of moral depravity. Unbelief is not so much the result of studious and controversial age as it is one of moral decline. It disperses itself in proportion as the general morals decline. People embrace it with less apprehension when all around are doing the same thing.[7]

The key to addressing spiritual sloth in our children is to empower them to take ownership of their convictions. Pascal advises, "So far from making it a rule to believe a thing because you have heard it, you ought to believe nothing without putting yourself into the position as if you had never heard it. It is your own assent to yourself, and the constant voice of your own reason, and not of others, that should make you believe."[8]

Casual conformity is far more dangerous spiritually than open rebellion. Parents must challenge their children's "whatever" attitude by increasing their sons' and daughters' intellectual responsibility for their own convictions, rather than decreasing their freedom to think for themselves. Our desire is conviction, not conformity; belief, not behavior. This requires a seeker's heart.

A SEEKER'S HEART

"The tragedy of modern man is not that he knows less and less about the meaning of his own life," writes Vàclav Havel, "but that it bothers him less and less."[9] Parents must encourage an attitude of seeking, as King David reminded his son: "And you, my son Solomon, acknowledge the God of your father, and serve him with wholehearted devotion and with a willing mind, for the LORD searches every heart and understands every motive behind the thoughts. If you seek him, he will be found by you" (1 Chronicles 28:9). A passionate truth-seeker has a wholehearted devotion and a willing mind. He or she doesn't know all the answers, but knows that the answers are important.

This is the opposite of indifference or sloth. An uncommitted agnostic is really a closet skeptic. Of them Pascal writes, "Those who do not love the truth take as a pretext that it is disputed, and that a multitude deny it. And so their error arises only from this, that they do not love either truth or charity. Thus they are without excuse."[10]

But seekers take truth so seriously that the search for it is their highest priority. Peter Kreeft observes, "The great divide, the eternal divide, is not between theists and atheists, or between happiness and unhappiness, but between seekers (lovers) and nonseekers (nonlovers) of the Truth (for God is Truth). Thus it is the heart and not the head that determines our eternal destiny."[11]

For many young people, however, money matters over meaning. The American Council on Education reports that college freshmen are more committed to financial success—75 percent—

than to developing a life philosophy—40 percent.[12] Herein lies our challenge—encouraging the attitude in our teenager of seeking truth passionately. The promise is clear: Only those who seek God find Him and all those who seek God find Him.[13]

A LOVER'S LONGING

Seeking is so crucial to finding because God wants willing hearts as much as convinced minds. He desires lovers, not philosophers. And so God does not communicate in a way that violates our freedom to love. He gives us clues that we must follow rather than conclusions to which we must submit. Knowledge requires that the seekers invest something of themselves. Again Pascal observes, "God wishes to move the will rather than the mind. Perfect clarity would help the mind and harm the will." He concludes, "Earthly things must be known to be loved, Divine things must be loved to be known."[14]

Likewise, in the Gospels Jesus revealed Himself in a way that was clear to those who were willing to follow, but confusing to whose who were not. "The secret of the kingdom of God has been given to you," He said. "But to those on the outside everything is said in parables so that, 'they may be ever seeing but never perceiving, and ever hearing but never understanding.'"[15]

Creating a spectacle was the temptation put to Him by the devilish marketing expert in the wilderness: "The devil led him to Jerusalem [the religious and cultural capital] and had him stand on the highest point of the temple. 'If you are the Son of God,' he said, 'throw yourself down from here'" (Luke 4:9). The Devil was advising, "Create a public relations event. Then everyone will automatically know who you are. Put it in lights! Get the Goodyear blimp!" Even Jesus' unbelieving brothers questioned His behavior, "No one who wants to become a public figure acts in secret. Since you are doing these things, show yourself to the world" (John 7:4). And yet again and again we see Jesus counseling those He has healed not to tell anyone.[16]

Jesus wants lovers, not paparazzi. He communicated through His hearers' wills, not in spite of them. So too God reveals Himself in clues that engage the passions of the true seeker. He gives undeniable clues, but the evidence of His existence does not so overwhelm us that we do not have to seek in order to find. Our minds follow our hearts.

The problem of understanding is calloused hearts; it's volitional before cognitive. Jesus says of those who did not recognize Him even as He stood before them, "For this people's heart has become calloused; they hardly hear with their ears, and they have closed their eyes" (Matthew 13:15). We see what we want to see, and we avoid seeing what challenges our assumed absolute autonomy. As Pascal puts it, "Ordinary people have the power of not thinking of that about which they do not wish to think."[17]

Only a communication strategy that demands our seeking is appropriate to His desire for our love. Søren Kierkegaard tells the parable of the "King and Maiden," which illustrates this beautifully. A powerful king fell in love with a humble maiden. He had no desire to ensnare her heart with potions or poetry because he desired her free love. Yet all around him were a crowd of "yes-men"—courtiers trained to tell him what he wanted to hear. In addition, statesmen who feared his political power overexuberantly sent congratulations for the nuptials. But in the king there grew a nagging doubt that he voiced to no one. For this was not a love of equals, but of unequals. Did the maiden love him for who and what he was or who and what he did? Was he loved for his person or for his power, his being or his benefits?[18]

God, like the king, wants our love. As we are unequals, He reveals Himself in disguise so that our hearts are not overwhelmed. Kierkegaard concludes, "Every other form of revelation would be a deception in the eyes of love."[19] Herein is the key: "He came to *give* light, as a gift, not to force light on us."[20] Perhaps one of the most poignant statements in the Bible is "Light has come into the world, but men loved darkness instead of light because their deeds were evil" (John 3:19).

Pascal summarizes the reason behind the requirement of a seeking heart:

If he had wished to overcome the obstinacy of the most hardened, he could have done so by revealing himself to them so plainly that they could not doubt the truth of his essence, as he will appear on the last day with such thunder and lightning and such convulsions of nature that the dead will rise up and the blindest will see him. This is not the way he wished to appear when he came in mildness, because so many men had shown themselves unworthy of his clemency, that he wished to deprive them of the good they did not desire. It was therefore not right that he should appear in a manner manifestly divine and absolutely capable of convincing all men, but neither was it right that his coming should be so hidden that he could not be recognized by those who sincerely sought him. He wished to make himself perfectly recognizable to them. Thus wishing to appear openly to those who seek him with all their heart, he has qualified our knowledge of him by giving signs which can be seen by those who seek him and not by those who do not. There is enough light for those who desire only to see, and enough darkness for those of a contrary disposition.[21]

There is nothing more important for our children than encouraging in them a humble attitude of passionate truth-seeking. The problem, as we have said, is not *finding,* but *seeking.* To paraphrase G. K. Chesterton, "Christianity has not been tried and found wanting. It has been unwanted and left untried."[22] Or as Winston Churchill quipped, "Men occasionally stumble over the truth, but most of them pick themselves up and hurry off as if nothing happened."

Seeking truth is what matters—for parents and children alike. "If we do not love the truth, we will not seek it. If we do not seek it, we will not find it. If we do not find it, we will not know it. If we do not know it, we have failed our fundamental task in time, and quite likely also in eternity."[23] We cannot be indifferent to spiritual indifference.

The challenge of parenting is to avoid coercing our convictions on our teenagers while encouraging them to take ownership of their beliefs. Feeling the weight and responsibility of their convictions will be the beginning of their spiritual pilgrimage. In their beliefs is the priority for our parental influence.

A Seeker's Priority

One of the ways I take advantage of e-mail is by sending periodic "Thoughts of the Day" to my teenage children in college and boarding school. Frequently these thoughts are Scripture references or quotations that have emerged out of my daily devotions. One day I sent the following single sentence by Dallas Willard: "We always live up to our beliefs."[24] A short time later I received a four-word response from David, my son at Colby College: "I wish I could." I responded in pithy e-mail fashion: "You do."

It is very easy to think that we can disconnect behavior from beliefs. But our children's beliefs are far more important than their behavior, for they will live out of their beliefs. If they seek the truth, their choice of beliefs will be changed. And if they seek something other than truth—pleasure or acceptance, for example—they will choose beliefs that to some degree are alienated from God and reality.

Satan's deception in Genesis 3 is to cause the woman to question reality as God created it: "Did God really say. . . . " Once the question is entertained, we are no longer on the same page with God. And yet we pretend that it is otherwise—that our beliefs are somehow better than our behavior. This pretense is the spirit of the antichrist: "They went out from us, but they did not really belong to us. For if they had belonged to us, they would have remained with us; but their going showed that none of them belonged to us" (1 John 2:19). John's warning is to watch what they do, and not what they say. This even goes for children: "Even a child is known by his actions, by whether his conduct is pure and right" (Proverbs 20:11).

Beliefs matter because beliefs control behavior; ideas have consequences. The overall pattern of our life choices is always based on our beliefs. Take a close look at your children's youth program at church. Too often they are an excuse for fun and games with little serious thinking or conscious planning for influencing beliefs at a crucial time of life. Consequently, it is not surprising that the behavior of Christian teens varies so little from their nonChristian friends. As Dallas Willard observes,

> When we bring people to believe differently, they really do become different. One of the greatest weaknesses in our teaching and leadership today is that we spend so much time trying to get people to do things good people are supposed to do, without changing what they really believe. . . . We frankly need to do much less of this managing of action, and especially with young people. We need to concentrate on changing the minds of those we would reach and serve."[25]

But how seriously do we take this important task?

In a day of "soccer moms" of hyperkinetic activity and labor, William Wilberforce's challenge to parents is amazingly contemporary:

> They would blush on their child's birth to think him inadequate in any branch of knowledge or any skill pertaining to his station in life. He cultivates these skills with becoming diligence. But he is left to collect his religion as he may. The study of Christianity has formed no part of his education. His attachment to it—where any attachment to it exists at all—is too often not the preference of sober reason and conviction. Instead his attachment to Christianity is merely the result of early and groundless prepossession. He was born in a Christian country, so of course he is a Christian. His father was a member of the Church of England, so that is why he is, too. When religion is handed down among us by hereditary succession, it is not surprising to find youth of sense and spirit beginning to question the truth of the system in which they were brought up. And it is not surprising to see them abandon a position, which they are unable to defend. Knowing Christianity chiefly by its difficulties and the impossibilities falsely imputed to it, they fall perhaps into the company of unbelievers.[26]

For Wilberforce, conscious religious instruction of our children is the starting point of real Christianity. "No one expects to attain to the heights of learning, or arts, or power, or wealth, or military glory without vigorous resolution, strenuous diligence, and steady perseverance. Yet we expect to be Christians without labor, study, or inquiry!" he laments.[27] "Christ wants a child's heart, but a grown-up's head," Lewis adds in *Mere Christianity*.[28] In contrast, what we prize in parenting is abundantly clear by looking in our wallets and Day-Timers.

If our desire is to influence our teenage children's beliefs, where do we begin? In the next chapter I suggest five aspects of how parents can encourage their children to become passionate seekers of truth.

CHAPTER SIXTEEN

The Lock and Key

PRIORITY:
Focus on Influencing Beliefs, Not Behavior

INFLUENCE AND INQUIRY

After we encourage an attitude of passionate truth-seeking in our adolescent children, the next issue we face concerns how we will influence these seekers. Again the key distinction is between influence and coercion: We must focus on shaping their beliefs rather than controlling their behavior.

A change in beliefs is always an indirect process; people only move to different beliefs when they are convinced that things are not what they once thought. This can happen in two ways. One is that they change their beliefs on the basis of influence.[1] That is, our beliefs are affected by those we trust; most of what we assume to be true we learn from others and simply accept on the basis of their authority. Conversely, if we question their authority, their influence weakens. Of course, one's influence doesn't make a thing true, but it does make it easier to believe.

Teens today are the first generation to have been raised without God. The challenge parents face is larger than just biblical literacy—it's plausibility. Religion rarely shows up on their radar screen as worthy of being believed. Rather, their convictions are largely based on those who have influence over them. The obvious question we should ask is, "Who has this influence?"

The other way beliefs change is on the basis of inquiry. Beliefs cannot be coerced; we have to be convinced for ourselves, not commanded by another. For example, my demand that you believe in extraterrestrial aliens will have little immediate influence on your beliefs. You might reasonably respond, "Prove it." We might then schedule a trip to Roswell, New Mexico, to look into the matter. Likewise with matters of faith: The seeker must be involved in an inquiry. Thus the second question is, "What is the nature of the inquiry?"

For parents to make a difference on the beliefs of their teenage children, they must be clued in on both accounts. We must be seen as those who have integrity in our behavior and intelligence in our beliefs. The Bible always combines both aspects: "But in your hearts set apart Christ as Lord. Always be prepared to give an answer to everyone who asks you to give the reason for the hope that you have. But do this with gentleness and respect, keeping a clear conscience, so that those who speak maliciously against your good behavior in Christ may be ashamed of their slander" (1 Peter 3:15-16).

Our answers are always connected to our actions. Our goal is not simply to be right; it is to make a constructive influence in their lives. "The bottom line," Patricia Hersch warns, is that "we can lecture kids to our heart's content, but if they don't care what we think, or there is no relationship between us that matters to them, or they think we are ignorant of the reality of their lives, they will not listen."[2]

Obviously, the influence on a teen's beliefs cannot be achieved in the absence of the other priorities we're already discussed. But five aspects for influencing beliefs are worth our examination: attractiveness, acceptance, applicability, answers, and alternatives.

1. Attractiveness

To influence our children's beliefs, our lives need to be winsome as they reveal the attractive reality of Christ in our lives. We will not have a positive effect if the spiritual reality our teenagers observe is a drag—a life-denying, joy-squashing list of "do's and dont's." Is the example of our life compelling to our children? Do they want to introduce their friends to us? Dick Keyes challenges,

> The goal is that our children should say, "I really *want* to walk in those footsteps." This is why it is so vital that the atmosphere of a family, each in its own unique way, must capture Jesus' affirmation of life. When they have a choice about it, most young people will not decide to subject themselves to a grim and joyless existence.[3]

Our walk with Christ should be a celebration of life and its richness. We do well to remember that Jesus' first miracle was to create 160 gallons of private-label reserve vintage at a wedding party. Celebration is a biblical spiritual discipline that is still practiced today by the Roman Catholic and Orthodox communities but long forgotten by the average evangelical. Many Christian parents need to let their hair down in a truly life-affirming Jewish pattern.

How else can we follow the Scriptures? The Israelites are commanded to participate in a regular celebration of God's gracious provisions: "Thou shalt bestow that money for whatsoever thy soul lusteth after, for oxen, or for sheep, or for wine, or for strong drink, or for whatsoever thy soul desireth: and thou shalt eat there before the LORD thy God, and thou shalt rejoice, thou, and thine household, and the Levite that *is* within thy gates" (Deuteronomy 14:26-27, KJV). As Dallas Willard writes, "This world is radically unsuited to the heart of the human person, and the suffering and terror of life will not be removed no matter how 'spiritual' we become. It is because of this that a healthy faith before God cannot be built and maintained without heartfelt celebration of his greatness and goodness to us in the midst of our suffering and terror."[4]

Imbued with meaning, filled with joy, and empowered by the Spirit—our lives must be a daily answering to the deadly culture of nihilism. Such an earthy spirituality gave Celtic Christians a powerful influence within pagan Ireland.[5] Such a life cannot be faked. Thus the strategy of influencing beliefs is much more demanding than the strategy of coercing behavior—which, of course, is why it is so little tried.

2. Acceptance

The second point is so simple that it hardly needs to be said, and yet it is indispensable: Parents must accept their children. What is so evident in the Gospels is how people were instinctively attracted to Jesus. And those most drawn to Him were those alienated and stigmatized by mainstream society. Jesus attracted the Goths and punks of His day more than the yuppies and jocks. He was winsome to the socially marginal and the morally questionable, those automatically despised by the religious people of His day. There can only be one explanation—Jesus did not have a condemning attitude.

When we condemn, we judge. When we judge, we distance ourselves. When we distance ourselves, we create a defensive dynamic in our relationships. And when there is a defensive dynamic, we will have no influence, for the door to the heart will be shut.

Influence begins with our attitude toward our children. Do they have the freedom to fail? Does our son feel rejected when we receive his poor report card? Does he feel condemned when the police arrest him for drugs? Does our daughter feel rejected when she admits to us that she is pregnant? Does she feel cast out when she is caught drinking? Our reactions to these real-life crises will determine how much influence we may have with our teenagers. Condemnation and influence are mutually exclusive.

Our children have years of experiences, beginning with the relatively trivial to the really traumatic, where we display either condemnation or acceptance. This doesn't mean accepting wrong behavior. But neither does it mean rejecting those who commit the behavior. The difference is pivotal. Dallas Willard's discussion of avoiding condemnation in our relationships deserves our close scrutiny:

> We do not have to surrender the valid practice of distinguishing and discerning how things are in order to avoid condemning others. We can, however, train ourselves to hold people responsible and discuss their failures with them—and even assign them penalties, if we are, for example, in some position over them—*without attacking*

their worth as human beings or marking them as rejects [emphasis added].[6]

This is not an easy distinction to maintain with our children, for it is too easy to take their failure as our own. But when we personalize their actions and overidentify with them, we will inevitably condemn. For the reality of Jesus in our lives to be the most evident, we must reject a spirit of condemnation. This is where the rubber hits the road in the life of a family—and particularly between a father and his teenage children.

3. Applicability

Third, our influence must be relevant in order to connect with our children's lives and thoughts. Here is where we reap the benefits of learning to understand their world. We see how Jesus' instruction was so different from other religious teachers in its lack of abstraction. He taught about kingdom life in terms of the concrete experiences of His hearers.

In contrast, one thinks of Emmanuel, the Barcelonan bellhop in the British sitcom *Fawlty Towers*. In one episode he exclaims proudly in his thick Spanish accent, "I speak English very well. I learned it from a book." And yet his minimal grasp of the language gets him in more trouble than knowing no English at all. Likewise, we cannot make the reality of the kingdom or the truth of Christianity applicable to our teenager if it is only "head knowledge"—something we "learned from a book." While we may have to do some serious reading ourselves, in the end, the truth we communicate must stem from the reality of our lives.

Moreover, we must realize that at times our teenagers will be in a place of uncertainty. The applicability of the Christian faith must be worked out in the ambiguity of their world, for Jesus taught about kingdom life in terms of our conscious experiences. Consequently, we must give our children the freedom to express their own confusion aloud.

Bertrand Russell was one of the most spirited champions of atheism in his day, writing such popular books as *Why I Am Not a Christian*. Later in life he reflected back on his adolescent years, which proved a pivotal turning point in his rejection of God.

> I became exceedingly religious and consequently anxious
> to know whether there was any good ground for supposing
> religion to be true. For the next four years a great part of
> my time was spent in secret meditation upon this subject.
> I could not speak to anybody about it for fear of giving
> pain. I suffered acutely, both from the gradual loss of faith
> and from the necessity of silence.[7]

The point of influence with our children is not our preconceived curriculum of instruction, but where their troubles and
doubts touch their lives. It is here—on the sensitive issues they
are least comfortable discussing—that the truth of the gospel
must be seen to be relevant. Our families need to be safe havens
where ideas can be exchanged freely, doubts safely expressed, and
even harebrained views tried out with impunity.

Sunday school classes and Christian schools rarely let one ask
skeptical questions with impunity. And so, as in the experience
of Bertrand Russell, the questions go unasked—and unanswered. Do we create an environment around our family dinner
table that allows all questions to be expressed without condemnation? When doubts are "dissed," certainty will not come.

After my senior year in college, I spent some time at L'Abri,
a community in Switzerland where people go to discuss the truth
and significance of Christianity. There, having the opportunity to
interact with the Christian apologist Francis Schaeffer and his
associates, I asked so many questions that most listeners assumed
I was a nonbeliever. But my searching probes were treated with
respect. The opportunity simply to put forth my queries helped
establish a new confidence in my relationship with Jesus.

As parents we must make the truth of the gospel relevant to the
real questions in our teenage children's lives. We do this by creating
an environment where questions are accepted and listening is the
rule. Many a father has said, "I don't understand my child; he won't
listen to me." But to understand our children's hearts begins with listening to them—and allowing them to express their confusion and
doubts. Only then can the truth of the gospel be applicable.

4. Answers

Fourth, we need to be prepared to answer honest questions with honest answers. Many of us find this aspect of influencing our children's beliefs difficult because we ourselves do not know *why* we believe *what* we believe. If we have never wrestled with the truth of our convictions, we will not be well-equipped to help our children.

Too many Christians accept Christianity for its psychological benefits before they are convinced of its philosophical truth. As C. S. Lewis warns,

> Foolish preachers, who are always telling you how much Christianity will help you and how good it is for society, have actually let you forget that Christianity is not a patent medicine. Christianity claims to give an account of the facts—to tell you what the real universe is like. Its account of the universe may be true, or it may not, and once the question is really before you, then your natural inquisitiveness must make you want to know the answer.[8]

In the midst of our deathwork culture, our apprenticeship to Jesus will stand or fall on whether we are fully convinced that He knows the truth about our lives. A faith without a foundation will not long stand.[9]

The Key to the Truth

Christianity is the key that unlocks the meaning of the universe and our existence. It makes sense of objective reality—both its beauty and brokenness. It brings clarity to who we are and to our deepest aspirations. For G. K. Chesterton, "Christianity was the answer to a very real riddle; it was not the last truism offered after a long walk."[10]

Pascal points out that much of what we know with *certainty* to be *true* we know apart from reasoning. "We know the truth not only by the reason but also by the heart. . . . Principles are intuited, propositions inferred, and all with certainty, though in different ways."[11] What Pascal is saying is that we know reality in two ways: some things we simply *intuit* apart from reason; other things, based on our intuitions, we *reason to*. When Pascal says, "the heart has its reasons, which reason does not know," he is not setting intuited knowledge over or against reasoned knowledge, but confirming the heart's way of knowing.[12]

In Pascal we find the balance we need to maintain certainty in a culture where reason has been cut off from reality. He writes, "If we submit everything to reason [modernity's rationalism], our religion will have no mysterious and supernatural element. If we offend the principles of reason [postmodernity's subjectivism], our religion will be absurd and ridiculous."[13] In this way we can come to grasp all of reality without the reductionism of either alternative.

A Christian worldview is reasonable, but it points finally to a relationship with Jesus. "Reason is like dating," writes Peter Kreeft, "faith is like marrying. How blind and foolish to marry someone you never dated and don't know!"[14] We are asked for more than reason; we are invited to make a commitment.

A Matter of Timing

There are two words of caution here to the overeager parent. The first regards the *timing* of our answers. Our children will only see our answers as their own when they have a real need. Answering unasked questions is often our well-intended but spiritually flawed way of trying to manage our children's beliefs. I must admit that I am prone to this temptation and have violated my own advice on many occasions.

Few words of Jesus are more important for a Christian parent to understand than these: "Do not give dogs what is sacred; do not throw your pearls to pigs. If you do, they may trample them under their feet, and then turn and tear you to pieces" (Matthew 7:6). Jesus is not saying that our teens are "swine," though some parents may be tempted by this interpretation. What he is suggesting instead is that we need to avoid manipulating our teenagers with "good" advice that has no *perceived* value to them and consequently is not *appreciated* by them.

The Tension of Unbelief

The second word of caution to the overeager parent relates to the *type* of answers we give. The truth of Christianity is not impersonal knowledge, but personal. It is not like the conclusion to a logical and reasoned argument (abstract) or the findings of a scientific experiment (impersonal), but more like the answer to a proposal of marriage (concrete and personal). It demands an involvement of the whole person—mind, emotion, and will. The truth of Christianity is found in its relation to life as we actually live it.

This was the secret of the late Francis Schaeffer when he encountered seekers at L'Abri. He wrote, "The truth that we let in first is not a dogmatic statement of truth of the Scriptures but the truth of the external world and the truth of what man himself is."[15] Although made in God's image to live in a world of His creation, people pretend that they can create their own rules. But people will always cheat—they acknowledge enough truth about God's world to remain human while abandoning enough to ensure freedom from moral responsibility.

Even the world's greatest atheist was aware of this basic dishonesty. Nietzsche wrote, "We godless anti-metaphysicans still take our fire, too, from the flame lit by a faith that is thousands of years old, that Christian faith, which was also the faith of Plato, that God is the truth, that truth is divine."[16] Those who have experienced the fire's reality uphold what Nietzsche once accepted before he put out the fire in his own heart. In contrast, when on November 23, 1654, Pascal met the living Christ, he wrote, "Fire. 'God of Abraham, God of Isaac, God of Jacob,' not of philosophers and scholars."[17]

Some cheat less; some cheat more. Those who cheat less are more honest but more despairing. Those who cheat more are more hopeful but more dishonest. Today many claim a sugarcoated nihilism—meaninglessness with a happy face. But when examined closely, the smile masks a smorgasbord of frenetic diversions designed to dull the pain of inevitable loneliness. Simon Reynolds acknowledges this deception within the teenage rave culture:

> From my double vantage point as fan and critic, participant and observer, darkside was a pivotal and revelatory moment: the life-affirming, celebratory aspects of rave were turned inside out, the smiley face torn off to reveal the latent nihilism of any drug-based culture. . . . The

dance floor was full of dead souls, zombie-eyed and prematurely haggard. Instead of outstretched arms and all-embracing extroversion, you'd see automaton/autistic body moves and vacant self-absorption. What started off as fun began to acquire the tinge of desperation.[18]

The tension of unbelief is first felt in life before in logic. This means that we may need to encourage our children to face the consequences of their unbelief before we encourage them to believe. Difficult as it may seem, we must allow them to test the waters of life without faith before they appreciate the need for having a rock upon which to stand.

Waking the Imagination

In addition, because our teenagers' hearts have been systematically constricted by the rationalism of secular education and the media, their imaginations may need to be expanded. This involves exposing them to great literature. For instance, it was through the romanticism of Wordsworth and the neopaganism of Yeats that C. S. Lewis became open to spiritual reality. He found in Yeats "an author exactly after my own heart."[19] He writes, "If he had been a Christian, I should have discounted his testimony, for I thought I had the Christians 'placed' and disposed of forever. But I now learned that there were people, not traditionally orthodox, who nevertheless rejected the whole Materialist philosophy out of hand."[20]

The same experience was true of Louise Cowan, editor of *Invitation to the Classics:*

Before literature came to my aid, I had perused theology in vain. Even the Bible was unconvincing. Not until a literary work of art awakened my imaginative faculties could the possibility of a larger context than reason alone engage my mind. . . . Above all else this seems to me the chief value of what we call the classics: they summon us to belief. They seize our imaginations and make us *commit ourselves to the self-evident,* which we have forgotten how to recognize.[21]

Great literature is heart surgery for the hardening of spiritual arteries. We do well to expose our children to those classics of literature that affirm the existence of truth.[22]

Clued In

A place to begin might be in watching and discussing the movie *Clueless* (1995). Loosely based on Jane Austen's *Emma*, the film depicts many of the complexities of modern teenage life, from finding out that one's boyfriend is gay to falling in love with one's visiting stepbrother. The lead character, Cher (played by Alicia Silverstone), is a popular Beverly Hills high schooler who seems preoccupied with conspicuous consumption—wanting, having, and wearing the latest LA style.

The movie's subtext is not about fashion, however, but about facing reality. Popularity, everpresent boyfriends, limitless credit cards, and unchecked freedom do not finally help her when she is forced to face her own selfishness. The real Cher is clueless, not because she is a dizzy blonde, but because she has never stopped the noise and nonsense long enough to examine the superficiality of her life.

Cher has buns of steel, a computer-coordinated designer ensemble to die for, a report card manipulated by the force of her personality, and popularity the envy of every girl in her zip code. But when life catches up with her, there is no one home—her soul is a neglected wasteland. Richard Foster writes, "Superficiality is the curse of our age. The doctrine of instant satisfaction is a primary spiritual problem. The desperate need today is not for a greater number of intelligent people, or gifted people, but for *deep* people."[23]

Both the timing and nature of answers are illustrated in Augustine's *Confessions*. During his youth Augustine followed a life of wild living and pagan philosophy. In the hope of correction and reformation, a devout widow befriended him and urged him to discuss his views with a learned bishop. But the bishop declined. As Augustine recounts,

> For he answered that I was still unready to learn, because
> I was conceited about the novel excitements of that heresy,

and because, as she had informed him, I had already disturbed many untrained minds with many trivial questions. "Let him be where he is," he said; "only pray the Lord for him. By his reading he will discover what an error and how vast an impiety it all is."[24]

This is painful but wise counsel. Influence cannot be forced.

5. Alternatives

Fifth, we must expose our children to the alternatives to faith. Our efforts to isolate our children from other worldviews will actually only serve to make them more suspicious of the truthfulness of Christianity. We need not be defensive, for the Christian faith can face all comers and shines brightest against its alternatives. G. K. Chesterton found this to be true, admitting that his return to faith was sparked when he encountered the other options: "It was Huxley and Herbert Spencer and Bradlaugh who brought me back to orthodox theology. They sowed in my mind my first wild doubts of doubt."[25]

Yale philosopher Nicholas Wolterstorff addressed the need for alternatives many years ago in his fascinating book concerning Christian education. In *Educating for Responsible Action* he explores what kind of education most reinforces the tendency toward moral behavior. An inarticulate positive moral example is important — the silent role model. But studies have shown that in isolation a negative moral example will have a stronger influence than a positive. A truly sobering finding of his book is that "it makes no appreciable difference whether models are presented *live* or by way of *representations* on film or television."[26] Put bluntly, the media trumps parents.

But what happens if one adds positive instruction to moral example? Instruction increases the tendency to moral behavior, but the relative strength of the convictions may not be as strong as we might imagine. Studies have shown again and again that pivotal to strong moral education is inoculation — a conscious exposure to alternative views. Wolterstorff concludes,

The best defense against attacks on the consensus (truisms) of one's community is inoculation—presenting and then refuting arguments against the elements of that consensus. Inoculation is far more effective than no defense at all, or reassuring defenses which never so much as mention objections. As [William J.] McGuire puts it: "A believer's faith in his culture's ideological truisms tends to have a spurious strength, analogous to the deceptive physical robustness of an animal brought up in a germ-free environment. Both are extremely vulnerable to attacking material and both gain resistance from pre-exposure to a weakened dose of the threatening material."[27]

In this regard, such books as Peter Kreeft's *The Journey: A Spiritual Roadmap for Modern Pilgrims* or James W. Sire's *The Universe Next Door: A Basic Worldview Catalog* and such curricula as The Trinity Forum's *The Journey: A Thinking Leader's Quest for Spiritual Meaning* are invaluable resources.[28] Kreeft, for example, provides a roadmap for choosing one's philosophy of life. He describes this pilgrimage as a series of ten life-choices: (1) Shall I question? (2) If I question, is there hope of answers, or should I be a skeptic? (3) If there is any objective truth, is there objective truth about the meaning of life? (4) If there is an objective truth about the meaning of life, is it that life is meaningless? (5) If life has real meaning, is it spiritual and not merely material? (6) If it is spiritual, is it moral? (7) If there is a real right and wrong, a real moral meaning, is it a religious meaning? (8) If there is a God, is God immanent (pantheism) or transcendent (deism)? (9) If God is both immanent and transcendent, are the Jews His prophet, His mouthpiece to the world? (10) If the Jews are God's prophet, is Jesus the Messiah?[29]

Sire, in turn, suggests that when we address the questions of life, we will only find seven basic questions and eight basic alternatives. The questions: (1) What is really real? (2) What is the nature of reality? (3) What is a human being? (4) What happens to a person at death? (5) Why is it possible to know anything at all? (6) How do we know what is right and wrong? (7) What is the meaning of human history? And the alternatives: Christian theism, deism, naturalism, nihilism, existentialism, Eastern pantheistic monism, new age, and postmodernism. He writes, "The fact is that we cannot avoid assuming some answers to such questions. . . . So long as we live, we will live either the examined or the unexamined life. It is [my] assumption . . . that the examined life is better."[30]

Such influence on matters as basic as belief requires that we respect the self-determination of our teenagers. We examine this aspect of parenting next.

CHAPTER SEVENTEEN

Out of Control

PRIORITY:
Respect Our Child's Self-Determination

NEUROTIC NURTURING

Chinese families, by government mandate, are limited to one child. This policy of enforced population control has unintended consequences, such as creating a society of spoiled only children (as well as an underground infanticide of female babies). State-sponsored antinatalism has led to an idolatry of children.

Within many Christian homes a similar idolatry is often present. The signs start early—from conception onward, nurturing becomes a consuming preoccupation that elevates both parental fear and expectations. The focus on hypercorrect child-rearing is usually well-intentioned, but it can easily slip into a form of neurotic nurturing that leads to inappropriate dependencies. Eventually, the child can become an extension of the parents' identity. When this happens, nurturing fulfills the parental need to be needed rather than the child's need to grow in independence.

Thus what looks like "perfect" parenting may actually be a form of suffocating enmeshment. When parents use money, gifts, promised inheritance, vacation homes, or other forms of manipulation to keep their children connected to them, they are showing signs of such an obsession. The high-hover mother can be just as destructive to the teenager's maturity as the phantom father.

If we follow the assumptions of much of the so-called Christian parenting advice, we would wonder whether the nineteenth-century missionary movement would have been possible. Again and again, missionaries put their children at risk for the sake of the gospel. For instance, when Amelia Taylor put her twenty-one-year-old son, Hudson, on board the little three-masted clipper *Dumfries* to sail to China in 1853, she never expected to see him again.[1] Years later in China he would write a friend in England, "I am striving to write a few lines from the side of a couch on which my darling little Gracie lies dying. . . . Dear brother, our heart and flesh fail, but God is the strength of our heart, and our portion for ever. It was no vain nor unintelligent act, when knowing the land, its people and climate, I laid my dear wife and darling children with myself on the altar for this service."[2]

What else does Jesus mean when He commands, "Anyone who loves his father or mother more than me is not worthy of me; anyone who loves his son or daughter more than me is not worthy of me; and anyone who does not take his cross and follow me is not worthy of me" (Matthew 10:37-38). Obedience to Christ is placed squarely in terms of our familial priorities.

The problem is not *what* we want as parents, but that we want it *too* much. If we idolize our children, Christ will not be first in our life. And such idolatry will keep us from placing Christ's purposes first in the life of our children. Christ demands that parents respect the self-determination of their teenager. The controlling grandmother played by Shirley MacLaine in the film *The Evening Star* (1996) is warned by her wise maid, "You can't live their lives for them." The family matriarch snaps back, "Neither can they." Letting our teenage children begin to live their own lives is the often painful challenge for parents and adolescents alike.

THE PRODIGAL PRINCIPLE

Jesus' parable of the prodigal son in Luke 15:11-38 is instructive as we consider the responsibility of parents to their teenage children. The familiar story concerns the younger son's rebellion and repentance and the father's loss and love. But even though we often focus on the rebellious youth, the central character in the story is the father himself. As a portrait of God's love, the prodigal's father gives a picture of emotionally healthy parenting. He sets the standard for the love our teenage children require.

Gleaned from the parable, the Prodigal Principle is this: Only unconditional love can give a prodigal child the freedom to leave; only unconditional love can offer a penitent child forgiveness to come home. The father respects the self-determining heart of his wayward son and lets him go even when he knows his decision is premature, offensive, unwise, and costly. Henri Nouwen writes,

> The father couldn't compel his son to stay home. He couldn't force his love on the beloved. He had to let him go in freedom, even though he knew the pain it would cause both his son and himself. It was love itself that prevented him from keeping his son home at all cost. It was love itself that allowed him to let his son find his own life, even with the risk of losing it.[3]

We can only truly appreciate the extent of this father's love when we realize what was culturally entailed in what his son was asking. The son's request broke with the father in four ways. First, it was a break with respect, for as the younger son, he did not have the prerogative to make demands on his father. We can see this culturally expected familial hierarchy illustrated in Genesis 27. Here Jacob sought his father's blessing through a complex deception to fool Isaac into thinking that he was his older brother.

Second, the prodigal's request was a break in relationship. To ask that the estate be divided prior to his father's death was in effect to say, "I wish you were dead." Acting on the father's will when he is still very much alive is to curse his life — it is to violate the material symbol of the bond between father and son.

Third, the request was a break with his responsibilities as a son. In a world without Social Security or retirement benefits, the father's savings were his only means of support. For the son to ask the father to dispose of his money — to sell off a third to half of his land and investments — was to break with his responsibility to care for his father in his later years.

Fourth, the son's request was a break with the family religion; he was severing any allegiance to the values and heritage that had been long instilled in his family. This is captured in the "distant country" to which he sets off. Nouwen expands, "He speaks about a drastic cutting loose from the way of living, thinking, and acting that had been handed down to him from generation to generation as a sacred legacy. More than disrespect, it is betrayal of the treasured family and community."[4]

The son's request was not just inconvenient and unwise, but a frontal assault on the dignity of the father. The prodigal intended not only to head out of town, but to hurt those he left behind. Despite this, the only authority the father claims is the authority of compassion. "That authority comes from letting the sins of his children pierce his heart," Nouwen concludes.[5] And so must we.

Under these circumstances, it is remarkable that the father just let his son go. But this kind of costly love is what is required of us with our teenagers. "Our children must experience that we are *for* their growing up, not against it, dragging our feet at every new freedom," Dick Keyes explains.[6] We must progressively give our teenagers the freedom to make decisive choices that affect their lives—even if everything in us screams against this.

Often in our panic to avoid a prodigal child, we do everything we can to ensure a compliant child. We much prefer the older brother to the younger. But the parable is clear that both sons were just as far away from accepting their father's love. Filled with self-righteous pride, the older brother sought to earn his father's love. Filled with self-centered lust, the younger brother sought substitutes for his father's love. In the end, the older brother's pride turned out to be an even larger obstacle than the younger brother's lust. This is because pigsty moments come easier to those who freely face the consequences of their rebellion than to those who mask their rebellion under a socially acceptable pretense.

EMOTIONAL UMBILICAL CORDS

As parents of teenagers we must sever the emotional umbilical cords. Some mothers never take this step because of their fear that they will no longer be needed. Susan Sarandon in the film

Stepmom (1998) plays a divorced mother who has no separate life or identity apart from her children. As the film ends, she is dying of cancer. On what will probably be her last Christmas with her children, she gives a present to her young son that symbolizes her relationship with him. It's a magician's cape on which she has sewn a photograph of her with him as a newborn infant. Her comment about the picture is a poignant example of overconnected parenting: "This is our first picture as *a couple* [emphasis added]."

As psychiatrist David Gutmann counsels, "The psycho-umbilical tie to the mother is crucial at the beginning of life, but it must, at some critical point, be severed."[7] For where the maternal instinct is not finally abandoned, C. S. Lewis warns, "the ravenous need to be needed will gratify itself either by keeping its objects needy or by inventing for them imaginary needs. It will do this all the more ruthlessly because it thinks that it is a Gift-love and therefore regards itself as 'unselfish.'"[8]

Many mothers are emotionally married not to their husbands, but to their children. Such a pattern is not only destructive to the institution of marriage but to the lives of the children. Teenagers, as young adults, must be permitted to live their own lives and face the stark consequences of their own choices.

This process of progressively taking ownership of one's life is what growing up is all about. "The teen years are the first time you make choices for yourself and get to know yourself by the choices you make," says seventeen-year-old Sarah Parnell.[9] Or as thirteen-year-old Lisa Briggs adds, "Having my opinions respected and often acted upon is the greatest gift my parents have given to me. . . . It's like even when they say 'no,' they're on my side. . . . They don't act like they own us."[10]

There is a world of difference between parents assuming the responsibility for influence and foregoing the temptation to control. "Successful parenting is the rightful, God-ordained loss of control," concludes Paul Tripp. "The goal of parenting is to work ourselves out of a job. The goal of parenting is to raise children who were once totally dependent on us to be independent, mature people who, with reliance on God and proper connectedness to the Christian community, are able to stand on their own two feet."[11]

Well-meaning parents too often cross the line between

influence and identity as they seek ways of living through their children. The dad who makes his love conditional on some type of achievement differs not from the mother who will not let the child out from under her wing. Both fail to respect the self-determination of the child.

In the film *Stepmom*, when the father's new girlfriend (played by Julia Roberts) challenges Susan Sarandon's overconnected parenting style, the mother responds incredulously, "You haven't been here from the beginning, worrying if every minute of every day that decisions you make are going to shape the people they are going to be." But she's wrong, because in the end it is not the parents' decisions that finally shape the child, but those of the child.

Beliefs, education, and friends are three basic areas where teenagers will begin to assume greater independence from their parents. Here especially the decision of parents to assert influence instead of control is paramount. For these three areas reveal what is true about who our teens are as self-determining individuals made in the image of God. We will examine beliefs and education in this chapter and friends and neighborhood, because of their important role, in the next.

PERMISSION TO DISAGREE

Should parents make their teenage child participate in the activities of faith—family devotions, youth group, church attendance, and Christian camps—when they have decided against God? In a word, no. Christianity is not about outward conformity but about freely following Christ. If one is uncertain, confused, or uncommitted to Christ, nothing is worse than being forced to pretend otherwise. Dallas Willard warns, "Forcing religion upon the young even though it makes no sense to them is a major reason why they 'graduate' from church about the same time they graduate from high school and do not return for twenty years, if ever."[12]

As we have seen in preceding chapters, our teenage children need to begin to assume greater personal responsibilities for their beliefs. This means that we must respect their decision if they, for whatever reasons, choose against our beliefs. This does not mean we shun them from family activities or stop talking to them about our points of disagreement; rather, we do not force them into situations that violate their consciences. As we continue respectful dialogue and debate, we also allow them to live with the consequences of their decisions.

At issue is whether we believe God can work in the lives of our children, whether we believe Christianity is able to withstand the harshest scrutiny, and whether we accept that our children will have to choose their own destiny. Dick Keyes writes,

> Christian parents will want to encourage their child to trust in Christ, but the trust must be the *child's* trust, not the parents' imposed veneer. That means that parents must encourage freedom of thought, welcoming questions, doubts, and difficulties by taking them seriously. Taking them seriously means hours of listening, admitting when they do not know an answer, and trying to discover answers together.[13]

Christian philosopher J. P. Moreland even goes further, adding, "I once told my children that if they ever got to the point where they thought it was unreasonable to believe that Christianity was true, then they should abandon the faith."[14]

This was the approach Francis Schaeffer took with his children at L'Abri. In the midst of the intellectual ferment of the sixties, the Schaeffer children were exposed in the home and in their Swiss classrooms to the alternatives to orthodox belief. When one of his daughters announced that she no longer believed Christianity was true, Dr. Schaeffer calmly respected her decision. She was told that she would still be treated as a member of the family but would not be expected to attend the family devotions at home or the worship at church. Faced with the weight of her own convictions, she wrestled with her questions and eventually returned with a deepened personal conviction of the love and truth of Jesus Christ.

Catholic apologist Luigi Giussani tells the story of a young man who came to him for confession, urged on by his mother. The man basically had no faith, and in the midst of the ensuing discussion, he laughed and said,

Listen, all that you are trying so forcefully to tell me is not worth as much as what I am about to tell you. You cannot deny that the true grandeur of man is represented by Dante's Capaneus, that giant chained by God to Hell, yet who cries to God, "I cannot free myself from these chains because you bind me here. You cannot, however, prevent me from blaspheming you, so I blaspheme you." This is the true grandeur of man.[15]

Giussani admits being unsettled by his outburst, but responded calmly, "But isn't it even greater to love the infinite?"[16]

Hell is the extent of God's respect for our self-determination. C. S. Lewis would have us remind our teenagers that "There are only two kinds of people in the end: those who say to God, 'Thy will be done,' and those to whom God says, in the end, 'Thy will be done.'"[17] The choice is our children's. "The ultimate rejection that should make us weep is not that they have rejected us, but Him."[18]

EDUCATIONAL CHOICE

Should parents give their teenage children the freedom to choose the type of school in which they pursue their education? Parents have a range of options when considering where to send their children to school, whether homeschooling, public schools, Christian private schools, parochial schools, or independent private schools (day and boarding). In addition, parents may have a range of choices based on their geographic area and financial capabilities.

Where we send our teenagers to school is a matter of grave significance to our children, for high school is the social institution of adolescence. This is why changing locations can be so difficult for a teenager. This decision is more than a matter of educational opportunities or extracurricular choices; school choices are usually about the choice of friends.

"What do you like most about school?" I asked an energetic middle-school student. "Lunch and recess," was the immediate response. "School is about friends," Patricia Hersch explains. "Even though many hate school, it is the happening place."[19] Or as Amy, a high-school metalhead, says, "My favorite times of the day are before school and after school, because that's when I hang around with my friends." Tracy adds, "I like the classes for who's in the classes, not for what we do in the classes. I like classes my friends are in."[20]

Parents may be thinking education, but kids are thinking friends. Parents may be thinking future, but kids are thinking fun. Judith Harris writes, "To children in school, the most important people in the classroom are the other children. It is their status among their peers that matters most to them—that makes the school day tolerable or turns it into a living hell."[21]

I visited a prestigious but small independent K-12 school in California that was having trouble retaining its middle schoolers. The issue was put bluntly by a seventh-grade boy, "No chicks and no cars." Educational quality could not compensate for the lack of a critical mass of students. In the next chapter we will discuss the role of friends in our teenager's life, but we should say now that when weighing decisions regarding schooling we must consider how important friends are to our teens.

Without some sense of ownership in their education, teenagers will frequently resist the educational opportunity offered. Educators agree on the fundamental fallacy of mandatory education. Dallas Willard observes, "The very idea of 'compulsory education,' of forcing young people to be in school—except where, very wisely and gently, quite small children are concerned—illustrates this misguided practice of pushing valuable things on people."[22]

Education involves the embodiment of knowledge. Facts and formulas must be personally ingested and made one's own. Great teachers may inspire, but when all is said and done, learning remains hard work—work that no one can do for students but the students themselves. Like the acquisition of a muscular physique or a perfect tan, learning cannot be done secondhand.

Thus, educational success cannot be achieved apart from the active participation of the child. Whether one is considering home-school or public school, Christian or secular, day or boarding, the teenager's input must be involved in the final decision. Few decisions have more potential for creating long-term resentment toward parents.

Consider the story of Jennifer, a sixteen-year-old home-schooled student in Loudoun County, Virginia. Her well-meaning Mennonite parents consistently resisted her pleas to attend public school. Depressed, Jennifer ran away from home several times, vandalized her room, and finally drew a knife on her father. At this point, the police became involved. A Loudoun County juvenile court subsequently ruled against the parents in favor of the child's choice to attend public school. Jennifer explained to the *Washington Post*, "They just wanted me to be sheltered for the rest of my life. . . . They need to let go. I'm to the age where I have to start making some decisions for myself."[23]

The point of the story is not to put homeschooling parents in a bad light—I've mentioned before my ties to the homeschooling movement. In fact, Jennifer's parents say they turned to home-schooling not to isolate her, but to give her more options. But while she did perhaps have a wider range of educational choices, she did not have the one choice that mattered most to her.

As parents our goal should be to give teenagers increasing responsibility for the decisions that shape their lives and reflect their hearts. There are no hard-and-fast rules that can be applied to every situation or child. But the principle of influence suggests that parents must find ways to respect the progressive self-determination of their teenager in their basic beliefs and in their educational choices. Closely related to both is the often contested choice of friends.

The Divine Majority

PRIORITY:

*Recognize the Influence of Peers
and Neighborhood*

THE SOUL SELECTS

Emily Dickinson's "The Soul Selects Her Own Society" is one of her most popular poems and is variously interpreted:

> The Soul selects her own Society—
> Then—shuts the Door—
> To her divine Majority—
> Present no more—
>
> Unmoved—she notes the Chariots—pausing—
> At her low Gate—
> Unmoved—an Emperor be kneeling
> Upon her Mat—
>
> I've known her—from an ample nation—
> Choose One—
> Then—close the Valves of her attention—
> Like Stone—[1]

Dickinson here is often considered to be commenting on Matthew 7:7: "Ask and it will be given to you; seek and you will find; knock and the door will be opened to you."[2] Her poem is seen as a metaphor of the lyrical self in search of its identity. But what is of particular interest for us is the process the soul takes in selecting its own society. Choosing one's friends is the greatest sign of the heart's direction and is therefore of key importance to us as parents of teenagers.

Dickinson provides several insights into the workings of the human heart in its relation to others. First, it is the soul that selects. We often talk about the problem of peer pressure when referring to teenagers, but it is actually more accurate to speak of peer preference. Rather than being coerced into a social group, the soul selects those whose loves and lifestyle match its own. In the words of one child psychologist, "Teenagers are not pushed to conform— they are pulled, by their own desire to be a part of the group."[3]

Second, once selected, this "society" becomes the person's "divine majority": the trump card of authority; the definer of the rules; the main players in the game. As C. S. Lewis observes, friendship always involves insiders and outsiders:

> Every real friendship is a sort of secession, even a rebellion.
> It may be a rebellion of serious thinkers against accepted
> clap-trap or of faddists against accepted good sense; of real
> artists against popular ugliness or of charlatans against civ-
> ilized taste; of good men against the badness of society or of
> bad men against its goodness. In each knot of friends there
> is a sectional "public opinion" which fortifies its member
> against the public opinion of the community in general.[4]

Third, Dickinson describes the soul as having a door, a low gate, and a mat. These may be humble descriptions, but we shouldn't be fooled by them. Once the door is shut, the soul is potentially impervious to outsiders, whether those who make a pretense of being invited (the "chariots" or carriages—those who just happen to drive by) or those whose presence implies power and privilege of access (the "Emperor"—those who kneel to be let in). And although there are many societies—an "ample nation"—from which the soul can choose, there is a narrowing of attention once chosen, after which the door to the soul closes.

The walls go up and what was once a door becomes like stone.

We all have witnessed this process with our teenagers at some point or another. The biblical advice is to be patient and gentle: to ask, seek, and knock rather than trying to force the door open. Our aim is to earn the right of passage to that soul and to be included in the child's divine majority. Dallas Willard describes the goal: "What position is nobler than that of a spiritual father who claims no authority and yet is universally esteemed, whose word is given only as tender advice, but is allowed to operate with the force of law."[5]

PEER POWER

Peer friendships are a hot topic in child psychology these days. Recent scientific research has undermined the key assumption of nearly forty years of child psychology, that parental nurture is the most important factor in a child's personality development and character formation. Many scholars are now debating this long unquestioned premise in favor of a growing awareness of the pivotal role of a child's friendships.

This view is expounded in Judith Harris's controversial but important new book, *The Nurture Assumption.*[6] We cannot dismiss her findings flippantly, for they are carefully backed by scholarly research and have the support of leading child psychologists at numerous prestigious universities and research foundations.[7] She presents the group socialization theory, which suggests that "children identify with a group consisting of their peers, that they tailor their behavior to the norms of the group, and that groups contrast themselves with other groups and adopt different norms."[8]

It has long been recognized that approximately half of what influences children's personalities stems from parental genes; the other half comes from the environment. What Harris's study seeks to evaluate is which environment shapes children's futures most decisively. Her controversial finding is that the long-term impact on their personality and behavior is not the environment that they share with their parents, but the one they share with their peers.[9] In short, peers trump parents. Harris writes, "The world that children share with their peers is what shapes their behavior and modifies the characteristics they were born with, and hence determines the sort of people they will be when they grow up."[10]

Harris is not claiming that parents have *no* influence, but she does say, in effect, that the heart's direction of young adults is best evidenced in their peer associations. Friends are destiny, not because friends control one's destiny, but because friends reveal one's heart, which in turn controls one's destiny. Christian clinical psychologist Margaret Alter explains, "Harris envisions and describes a child far more active, observant, intelligent, resilient, and flexible than the more passive, acted-upon infant we are accustomed to meeting in the psychology of popular culture."[11] In short, Harris's research validates the premise behind the influence paradigm discussed in this book—the self-determination of the child.

Many others have held similar views. For instance, in 1966, James Coleman observed that an important part of children's school environment consists not in the physical facilities of the school, the curriculum, or the teachers, but in their fellow students.[12] Or in a study of prep-school culture, educator Arthur Powell acknowledges, "The composition of any school's student body is a powerful educational force. It often determines whether or not a school becomes a descent community or an educational one."[13] Much earlier, Emerson wrote, "You send your boy to the schoolmaster, but 'tis the schoolboys who educate him."[14]

After Patricia Hersch's three years following eight teenagers she observed, "Whatever behavior is common to a group of kids feels normal to them, whether it be doing drugs or doing homework. Whether the adult world sees the lifestyle as positive or negative is not the standard kids are using." She concludes, "The family is not a powerful predictor of adolescent choices."[15] Or as Gregory Bodenhamer warns, "Who your children spend their time with in large part determines their attitudes, values, and behavior patterns. The most potentially dangerous (or helpful) people your children are ever going to associate with are their friends."[16]

But wherein lies the danger? Are friends the cause or the consequence of the problem? As parents we may not like what we see in the behavior or character of our children's friends. But of even greater concern should be what the choice of these friends reveals about their character and thus their heart. Providing influence at that level, rather than focusing on what follows, must continue to be our priority.

For example, we know that we are supposed to talk to our children about sex. But do we talk with equal seriousness to them about their choice of friends? How many sermons do we hear on the importance of choosing friends wisely? It seems a surprising omission, in that the Bible strongly underscores Harris's emphasis on the power of peers.

PROVERBS ON PEERS

Proverbs is full of practical wisdom on friends: "He who walks with the wise grows wise, but a companion of fools suffers harm" (Proverbs 13:20). Friendships are never based solely on context or coincidence, but choice. They always illustrate the deeper priorities of our lives. Proverbs 24:21-22 says, "Fear the LORD and the king, my son, and do not join with the rebellious, for those two will send sudden destruction upon them, and who knows what calamities they can bring?"

Knowing that music is often a reflection of teenage identity, we can say with some confidence, "Show me your CDs and you have bared your soul." The same is true of friends. This is why "A righteous man is cautious in friendship, but the way of the wicked leads them astray" (Proverbs 12:26).

C. S. Lewis observes, "The dangers of friends are perfectly real. Friendship can be a school of virtue; but also a school of vice. It is ambivalent. It makes good men better and bad men worse."[17] Friends may reinforce or exaggerate the directions of the heart, but they only unveil the hidden truth of who we really are. It is far easier to blame our children's friends for their behavior than to admit honestly what their choice of friends reveals about the state of their soul. Bad friends are a symptom of a problem, but not usually the cause.

PRIORITIES OF PARENTS

What can we do to influence the direction of our teenagers' choice of friends? As we have said before, influence cannot be achieved apart from the parental priorities of the preceding chapters. But we can add several additional considerations.

Because the neighborhood and the school eclipse the home as the primary sites for socialization, parents will have a primary influence on their children through the neighborhood they live in and the school environment they select.[18] Thus Judith Harris found that the parents' choice of their child's peer group (their school) and of the parents of the child's peer group (their neighborhood) are by far the most decisive decisions that parents make in their child's development.

Who Is My Neighbor?

Parents often move to neighborhoods where the presence of other children is evident. For instance, when young parents purchase a home, they look for all the telltale signs of potential friends for their children—tricycles, bikes, and basketball hoops. But it is less common for prospective homeowners to know the other parents in the neighborhood. With today's high degree of social mobility and dual-income families, it is not uncommon for parents to know little about their next-door neighbors, much less those down the street. And yet, Harris found that the neighborhood parents have as much influence over our children as we do within our own home. Children's peer associations inevitably become the primary sites of their formation.

Parental influence is context specific. "A parent's behavior toward a child affects how the child behaves in the presence of the parent or in contexts that are associated with the parent," Harris discovered.[19] Normative behavior in our home is not guaranteed outside of it. For example, if television is avoided in the home to minimize its negative influence, one's child will still be affected because of the impact of television in the neighborhood peer group.

Homeschoolers should take note: "The child whose home life is odd in some way, because he isn't permitted to watch television or because his parents are different from the other parents on the block, will nonetheless acquire the same culture as his peers. He gets it in the same place his peers get theirs: in the peer group."[20] In general, parental influence does not translate outside the home unless the child's peer associations reinforce the perspectives of the parents.

Thus the generalized values of the parents in the neighborhood become the baseline for the values of the children in the neighborhood. Harris concludes, "Kids (as a group) tend to behave like the adults in their village or neighborhood. It isn't because individual kids are behaving like their own parents. If heredity is not involved, kids are as similar to their friends' parents as they are to their own."[21]

Where we decide to live should be a self-conscious decision as it has a direct bearing on our children's long-term development. We would do well to remember C. S. Lewis's advice to a friend, "Friendship is the greatest of worldly goods. Certainly to me it is the chief happiness of life. If I had to give a piece of advice to a young man about a place to live, I think I should say, 'sacrifice almost everything to live where you can be near your friends.'"[22]

What Is the Character of the Student Body?

A second way parents can influence their children's peer associations is through the school their teens attend. School size and the character of the student body are of particular importance. Harris found what most parents know by common sense: "American children tend to learn more in classrooms that have few students. The reason may be that it is easier for the teacher to make a smaller class into a united group. The kids are less likely to divide up into contrasting groups with contrasting attitudes toward schoolwork if there aren't very many of them."[23] More than the quality of instruction, parents need to be concerned with the character of those who will be around their children. The larger the school—drawing from more diverse neighborhoods—the greater the negative peer group options available.

In the past thirty years, public high schools have grown bigger and more impersonal, doubling in size. We have megamalls, and now we have mega-high schools—with more educational and extracurricular alternatives as well as more social problems. Economist Robert J. Samuelson observes, "In 1950 almost 25,000 public high schools had 5.7 million students. In 1995 fewer than 24,000 had 12.5 million."[24]

Consider the experience of two students. The first, sixteen-year-old Lucy Smith, attended a small, elite prep school. But as she started her sophomore year, her four best friends left for different schools. With the loss of them the prospect of staying was no longer as attractive. Shortly thereafter her father died unexpectedly. She decided to make a change and attend a large public school. A year later she looked back on the decision and the difference between the environments at the two schools:

> There seems to be more sexual tension in the halls than at my old school, which was more like a family because people knew each other for so long and shared a lot of the same values. . . . It might seem strange that I would leave an environment that was so nurturing for a much more unsafe and erratic place, but I felt suffocated by the familiarity of my old school and weighed down by the competitive pressure.[25]

The new school provided her the opportunity for more freedom and greater anonymity.

In contrast, Keith Harris, age eighteen, left a large public school in Washington, D.C. to attend a private prep school. Of his former school he writes, "My old school district, the H. D. Woodson High School, is in the middle of about five different ghettos, and all of these neighborhoods don't like each other, so it's a bit like a war zone."[26] The tensions of the neighborhood cultures found their way into the hallways of the school and shaped its culture.

In fact, the dominant peer culture of a school will be determined by the majority subculture of those attending the school. Thus when checking out a school, parents need to ask school administrators more than simply what are the educational and extracurricular offerings. Parents need to inquire about the culture of the school—the character of the student body and its degree of fragmentation or unity.

How Does One Make New Friends?

Parents can make a significant contribution to their children's peer associations by sending them to Christian camps. More than one parent has commented on the valuable friendship their teenager has made by participating in summer camping programs such as those available through Summit Adventures in California, Young Life in Colorado, Deerfoot Lodge in New York, or FOCUS camps on Martha's Vineyard, Massachusetts. The combination of spiritual input and new friendships make these experiences fruitful opportunities for teenagers to reevaluate their lives and direction. Indeed, it was after being invited by a friend to a Christian retreat that Cassie Bernall accepted Christ and turned her life around before tragically becoming a Christian martyr at the Columbine High School massacre.[27]

We should endeavor to promote every opportunity for good friends and associates for our teenagers, for we are eventually unable to determine their selection of friends. The day comes when control is both inappropriate and usually impossible. For instance, I have been emphatic with my teenage children about the potential heartache involved in their dating nonbelievers. Eugene Peterson makes the point clearly in his paraphrase of the New Testament:

> Don't become partners with those who reject God. How can you make a partnership out of right and wrong? That's not partnership; that's war. Is light best friends with dark? Does Christ go strolling with the Devil? Do trust and mistrust hold hands? Who would think of setting up pagan idols in God's holy Temple? But that is exactly what we are, each of us a temple in whom God lives. (2 Corinthians 6:14-16, MSG)

But, of course, if a parent has to make this point too strongly or too often, then the problem is their teenager's relationship to Christ, not who they are dating. If they are serious about following Christ and living on the basis of His kingdom resources, then these secondary matters will usually take care of themselves. We need to provide influence where possible while always keeping first things first.

CHAPTER NINETEEN

For Our Child,
Like a Child

PRIORITY:
*Pray for Our Child as Our First
Responsibility*

FIRST THINGS LAST

Ironically, the last priority of parenting is really the first. Yet to our overly secularized and therapeutically conditioned ears, its admonition sounds almost trite: The principal responsibility of parents is to pray for our children. Prayer is such a given of discipleship that we may think it hardly needs mentioning. But doesn't it? Sadly, our spiritual practice belies its foundational nature.

The first things of parenting are not horizontal, but vertical. Before learning to communicate with our children, we must learn to converse with our Father. As important as spending time with our children is spending time on their behalf on our knees. Theophan the Recluse, a nineteen-century Russian Orthodox Bishop, wisely counseled: "Prayer is the test of everything; prayer is also the source of everything; prayer is the driving force of everything; prayer is also the director of everything. If prayer is right, everything is right. For prayer will not allow anything to go wrong."[1]

I think we can safely say that the measure of our maturity in Christ is found in the depth of our prayer life, for the secret places of the heart reveal the nature of our relationship with Jesus. For many, prayer is merely lip service, not a lifeline. Our money and our hymns may say "In God We Trust," but if we are honest we know better. We put our trust in a host of other things—education, employment, health, savings, and perhaps even the government.

Few of us have had all of our earthly securities removed. For most people such an experience would feel like an enormous personal crisis because few of us actually rely on prayer and the promises of God alone. Too often prayer is an afterthought—after we reach for the cell phone to call our doctor, lawyer, broker, or therapist. This being the case, no wonder we see parenting teens as such a personal challenge. Seen biblically, parenting teenagers is one of the greatest opportunities we have to learn how to pray, putting to work our faith in God's faithfulness.

As I began writing this book a year ago, I simultaneously decided to make it my spiritual goal to learn everything I could about "listening prayer." I dutifully noted the goal in my FranklinCovey Planner and began reading everything I could find on the subject. I was in danger of becoming a walking encyclopedia. But soon my knowledge was put to the test as my wife and I found all our securities removed except Christ Himself—we literally lost our jobs, home, an automobile, and savings. The result was a year when we were forced to rely on the Lord more fully and pray more earnestly.

Never before has our faith been tested more completely. We are slowly—and painfully—learning to live on our true foundation. "If we are really trusting in Him and seeking from Him, we cannot be put to shame. If not, perhaps the sooner we find out the unsoundness of any other foundation, the better," Hudson Taylor wrote in a letter to his fellow missionaries in China, calling them to a day of prayer and fasting.[2] We specialize in building safety nets around our lives to protect our wealth and reputation, but in doing so miss out on the richness of trusting in God alone.

And so it is with our children, whose lives are increasingly lived under their own direction. Our role as parents rightly shifts from control to influence, as we have discussed throughout this book. Pivotal in our influence is our life of prayer—the first priority of parenting. Too often it becomes the final resort in times of adolescent crisis rather than remaining the daily work of godly parents. When, for example, was the last time you spent a day praying and fasting for your child?

LIKE A CHILD

Prayer always reminds us that we are children before a loving heavenly Father. Isaac of Nineveh wrote in the seventh century, "When you face God in prayer, become in your thought like a speechless babe. Do not utter before God anything which comes from knowledge, but approach him with childlike thoughts, and so walk before him as to be granted that fatherly care, which fathers give their children in their infancy."[3]

Prayer concerns the relationship of a father to a child. As we pray for our child, the roles are reversed for here we are the child and God is the parent. What is amazing is that the same love and concern that impels us to pray for our child—a love that only a parent can know—is the same love and concern that our heavenly Father has for us on an infinite scale. The One for whom "the nations are like a drop in the bucket," is the same One who "gathers the lambs in his arms" (Isaiah 40:15,11). In our heavenly Father, the circle of a parent's love is completed.

Critics warned Hudson Taylor and the other English missionaries to China that they risked being lost in that distant land, as they would be beyond the reach of "civilization." Hudson Taylor responded,

> Before long you may find yourselves without even the
> necessities of life! I am taking my children with me and
> I notice it is not difficult to remember that they need
> breakfast in the morning, dinner at midday, and supper at
> night. Indeed, I could not forget them if I tried. And I find
> it impossible to think that our heavenly Father is less ten-
> der and mindful of his children than I, a poor earthly
> father, am of mine. No, he will not forget us![4]

In the dynamic of that personal relationship, God listens to us just as we listen to our child. And as any good parent, He honors our requests when they are in our best interest. More than that, He wants us to ask Him; He wants us to need Him; He wants to show us His love. Our prayers are not spiritual games or a cosmic charade. Dallas Willard reminds us that our prayer matters—to God and to us. Prayer changes history.

Our requests really do make a difference in what God does or does not do. The idea that everything would happen exactly as it does regardless of whether we pray or not is a specter that haunts the minds of many who sincerely profess belief in God. It makes prayer psychologically impossible, replacing it with dead ritual at best. . . . His nature, identity, and overarching purposes are no doubt unchanging. But his intentions with regard to many particular matters that concern individual humans beings are not.[5]

Thus the heart of God is the heart of a parent. With such a God ready and willing to hear our requests, we do well to lift up our children regularly, specifically, and earnestly before Him.

LESSONS OF A WARRIOR

Few people have demonstrated a life of prayer more faithfully than Hudson Taylor (1832-1905). His medical and evangelistic work in China remain an inspiration to all who seek to further the kingdom of God. The principles of prayer that came to characterize his life and his China Inland Mission are especially applicable to us as we pray for our precious children.

Taylor knew both the cost of ministry and the burden of parenthood. He buried two young children in China and sent three others home to England for medical and educational reasons. Because he was separated from his children for long periods, his parental influence was often left to daily prayer and regular letters. His son, Dr. Howard Taylor, wrote *Hudson Taylor's Spiritual Secrets* in 1932, from which we gain six principles that we should reflect on as we pray for our teenage children.

1. It's God's work.

We would do well to remind ourselves that our direct role as parents is a temporary stewardship. The day will come when our children will embark on their own lives, leaving us to pray for them. We may deem this a secondary responsibility of parenting, but it's actually our primary responsibility both before and after our children leave.

As parents we participate in God's work in our child's life. It is, however, finally God's work. Hudson Taylor wrote, "Had not my mind been sustained by the conviction that the work is His and He is with me in what it is not an empty figure to call 'the thick of the conflict,' I must have fainted or broken down. But the battle is the Lord's, and He will conquer. We may fail—do fail continually—but He never fails."[6]

Our greatest comfort as parents is that God loves our children far more than we have loved them or ever will. He will never forget nor abandon them as they set out on their own path. We need to follow the example of Hannah, the mother of Samuel, who humbly turned her beloved son over to the Lord. To Eli, she said, "I prayed for this child, and the LORD has granted me what I asked of him. So now I give him to the LORD. For his whole life he will be given over to the LORD" (1 Samuel 1:27-28).

2. God alone is sufficient for God's own work.

The quickest test of our trust and reliance on our Savior is whether we are anxious, worried, or depressed—all emotions easily triggered by teenage children. In such times God's command is clear: "Ask and leave it to God." As Paul instructed the Philippians, "Do not be anxious about anything, but in everything, by prayer and petition, with thanksgiving, present your requests to God. And the peace of God, which transcends all understanding, will guard your hearts and your minds in Christ Jesus" (4:6-7).

Anxiety is a spiritual fever; a warning sign that our spiritual life is ill. Taylor wrote, "Let us see that we keep God before our eyes; that we walk in His ways and seek to please and glorify Him in everything, great and small. Depend upon it, God's work, done in God's way, will never lack God's supplies."[7] Peace that transcends our human understanding is possible only if we learn to walk by faith, not by sight. If our life must always make sense to us, then God need not be involved.

When the Israelite spies returned from Canaan, all twelve reported the same facts—a prosperous land with fortified cities. But where the majority differed from Caleb and Joshua was the way they interpreted what they saw (Numbers 13-14). While the ten were fearful of the people of great size, the minority of two counted on more than what met the eye, for they relied on God. They told the grumbling Israelites, "Do not be afraid of the people of the land, because we will swallow them up. Their protection is gone, but the LORD is with us" (Numbers 14:9).

What do we count on in our parenting? Communication skills? Emotional intelligence? Or the One who is sufficient—Christ? Like Joshua and Caleb, we need eyes that are open to the Unseen Real. Elisha, too, had these eyes of faith. When surrounded by hostile armies, he told his panicked servant, "Don't be afraid. . . . Those who are with us are more than those who are with them" (2 Kings 6:16). When the heat is on—a guaranteed part of parenting—we must remember to "fix our eyes on Jesus" (Hebrews 12:2).

3. God is the "One Great Circumstance of Life."

Often we are confused about the nature of reality. Notions of fate, karma, or "The Force" weaken our appreciation of what it means to live in an open universe: a place in which personhood matters; a place where people can change the course of history; a place where, as individuals made in God's image, we are invited to an intimate, personal relationship with the Creator of the universe.

At its deepest level the universe is Trinitarian; it is about relationships, not things. The dynamic that holds the whole universe together is the love of a personal God: "In him all things hold together" (Colossians 1:17). Or as Paul reminded the Greek philosophers of his day, "In him we live and move and have our being" (Acts 17:28). Reality is personal; reality is relational; reality is love. *Vocatus atque non vocatus, Deus Aderit*—"Invoked or not invoked, God is present."

And thus all things fall under the scope of His love. "And we know," Paul writes, "that in all things God works for the good of those who love him, who have been called according to his purpose" (Romans 8:28). The circumstances of our lives are not the product of an impersonal, chance universe, but are the provisions of a personal, providential God.

Early in his life Hudson Taylor learned "to think of God as the One Great Circumstance of Life, and of all lesser, external circumstances as necessarily the kindest, wisest, best, because they are either ordered or permitted by Him."[8] Nothing happens by accident—God is the God of all things and is intimately involved in the circumstances of our lives and those of our children. We pray, knowing that He is active and present in the details.

4. We must learn to move others by prayer alone.

As parents we are constantly tempted to seek to control our children's hearts. We call it love—we feel we know what's best—yet to our teenage children it feels like manipulation and coercion. As we have seen, a heart can be influenced but never controlled, for this is the way God works. Richard Foster in *Prayer: Finding the Heart's True Home* comments,

> This aspect of God's character—this respect, this courtesy, this patience—is hard for us to accept because we operate so differently. Some people frustrate us so much that sometimes we wish we could open up their heads and tinker around inside a bit. This is our way, but it is not God's way. His way is higher than our way. His way is like the rain and the snow that gently falls to the earth, disappearing into the ground as they nourish it. When the time is right, up springs new life. No manipulation, no control; perfect freedom, perfect liberty. This is God's way (Isaiah 55:8-11).[9]

God, through His Holy Spirit, addresses the heart in ways that no one else can. Thus we do well to learn to move others through prayer, allowing and pleading for God to work directly on their hearts. As a young man, Taylor acknowledged, "When I go out to China, I will have no claim on anyone for anything. My only claim will be on God. How important to learn, before leaving England, to move man, through God, by prayer alone."[10]

Conquer through Christ, for He can open any door, move any heart, and change any circumstance. This demands waiting and being silent. We must let God take control of the circumstance rather than preempting His timing or ways.

In the film *Deep Blue Sea* (1999), scientists in an underwater laboratory are about to undergo a dangerous escape in shark-infested waters. The cook/preacher takes the hands of the survivors and recites Psalm 23. But when he gets to the phrase "Even though I walk through the valley of the shadow of death, I will fear no evil," he adds, "For I will carry a big stick and kick butt. . . . " His "prayer" is less an affirmation of his reliance on God than it is a pep talk for self-reliance. So-called heroic action replaces humble asking.

5. Difficulties are the platform for grace.

Parenthood is life in a nutshell—it will always have its share of joys and sorrows. We are not promised that parenting will be easy or even that our best efforts will produce perfect children. "Difficulties," Taylor wrote, "afford a platform upon which He can show Himself. Without them we could never know how tender, faithful, and almighty our God is."[11]

What we are promised is that God is sufficient in our times of need. In difficult circumstances our faith grows as we witness the fact of God's sufficiency. Over time, we learn to trust and to place our troubles and our children in God's hands. We then are able to embrace difficulties as opportunities for God to act. "I am no longer anxious about anything for He, I know, is able to carry out His will, and His will is mine." Taylor adds,

> It makes no matter where He places me, or how. That is rather for Him to consider than for me, for in the easiest position, He must give me His grace, and in the most difficult His grace is sufficient. . . . If God should place me in great perplexity, must He not give me much guidance; in positions of great difficulty, much grace; in circumstances of great pressure and trial, much strength? No fear that His resources will be unequal to the emergency! And His resources are mine—for He is mine, and is with me and dwells in me.[12]

We must come to the place where we embrace the difficulties with our children for the spiritual blessings they can afford. Suffering can be redemptive; it can bring blessing. Oswald Chambers writes, "God does not give us overcoming life: He gives us life as we overcome."[13] Our trust in God's faithfulness does not grow on the mountaintop but in the valleys of life. Only here will we learn that, in the words of German hymnwriter Georg Neumarck, "God never yet forsook at need the soul that trusted him indeed."

6. God's answers are always just in time.

We can say two things about God's answers to our prayers: They are never early and they are never late. One of the management innovations borrowed from the Japanese—"just in time" manufacturing and inventory management—models this principle when at its best. Requiring a complex system of controls to implement successfully, the idea is to reduce the inventory of parts and finished products in order to lessen the amount of money tied up in passive storage. Ideally, every finished product is customized directly for the customer with minimal delay and maximum efficiency. Because of the capability of computers, the concept is being applied to everything from automotive manufacturing to textbook publishing.

God in His infinite wisdom is far more efficient than the most powerful Cray Supercomputer. His loving answers are the providential outworking of His just-in-time provisions. God knows what we need and will supply His answers when we need them—and not before. We, however, like a little cushion; we tend to keep some parts in storage and some inventory on the lot. But are we relying on our hoarded stockpiles or on His sufficiency? In times of trial and uncertainty, we do well to remember that God's answers are always just in time.

We can see Hudson Taylor's trust and faith in a bountiful God when he assumed responsibility of running the Ningpo Hospital after its founder returned to Scotland for health reasons. Over the course of several months the money and supplies dwindled. Dr. Taylor and his staff were much in prayer about the matter, but day after day went by without the expected answer. Then one morning, the cook rushed in to announce that he had opened the last bag of rice. Taylor replied, "Then the Lord's time for helping us must be close at hand." And so it was—before the bag of rice was finished their answer came.[14]

We aren't always so filled with faith. Our impatience with God is often rooted in our desire for answers to prayers *now*— before we really need them. We worry about the future and forget that God's promise is for daily bread and manna in the morning. For God desires that we trust Him in the present moment, confident that His provisions will always be sufficient to our daily need.

Of course, we will only be able to see God's hand at work if we wait on His timing. Too often we wait and then become impatient, taking matters into our own hands. Spiritual impatience—getting ahead of God, or worse, preempting Him—is a grave danger for which I, a can-do entrepreneur by temperament, am especially prone. In fact, I was once told that this is my "fatal flaw." My well-intentioned zeal can mask a failure to wait on the Lord's timing. So too with our children when we presume to know best while failing to wait until God has prepared their hearts.

Taylor, in a letter to a colleague in the China Inland Mission, shared a similar lesson he was learning as he waited on God's timing:

> It is no small comfort to me to know that God has called me to my work, putting me where I am and as I am. I have not sought the position and I dare not leave it. He knows why He places me here—whether to do, or learn, or suffer. "He that believeth shall not make haste." That is no easy lesson for you or me; but I honestly think that ten years would be well spent, and we should have our full value for them, if we thoroughly learned it in them. . . . Moses seems to have been taken aside for forty years to learn it. . . . Meanwhile, let us beware alike of the haste of the impatient, impetuous flesh, and of its disappointments and weariness.[15]

How the father of the prodigal son must have longed to hire detectives to search out the one he loved and bring him home. But he didn't. Instead he waited, prayed, and trusted in his heavenly Father for His timing and His own work in the prodigal's heart. God is not in a hurry, and frequently His timing is not our own. But the blessings come when we allow God to work in His own way, in His own time.

THE PLUSES

I recently had lunch with Joel Belz, CEO of *World* magazine. Our conversation turned to our children and to the parental pain of having a wandering child. He shared with me his experience with his daughter, Elizabeth, who left her Christian home as a teenager to run away with an older man. Two years later, after daily and tearful prayers by her parents, Elizabeth returned to them and to her church.

Joel told me of the many parents who have shared with him their similar stories of wandering teenagers. He then pulled out his daily planner with its list at the back of over forty-five teens he aims to pray for each day. Beside each name is a "plus" or "minus" sign to indicate whether the son or daughter has returned. Joel also mentioned how he had recently been in California with a much respected evangelical theologian, who also has a wandering daughter for whom he has been praying for more than two decades. When Joel showed the aging warrior of faith the list of names, his eyes filled with tears. And then a smile broke over his face and he said, "Look at all the 'pluses.'"

Our job is to pray—patient, particular, persevering prayer. At times we may become discouraged, as Richard Foster notes: "We can easily become disheartened by [the process of intercessory prayer]. I think Jesus understood this, and, as a result, he gave more than one teaching on our need for persistence. . . . He even specifies his reason for telling these stories, namely, that we would 'pray always and not . . . lose heart' (see Luke 18:1)."[16] As the Lord told the apostle Paul, "My grace is sufficient for you, for my power is made perfect in weakness" (2 Corinthians 12:9).

The loving prayer of a parent is a prayer that is dear to the heart of God, for it mirrors His love for us. It is God's faithfulness that allows us to parent without anxiety—and frankly, without perfection. For where we fail, His faithfulness remains.

"Absalom! Absalom!"

THE PALACE TABLOIDS

The story of King David and his son Absalom is a sobering way to end a book on parenting. But it serves to remind us of two unforgettable lessons: First, our children tend to follow in our sinful behavior; and second, our children are the context where we learn the heart of God.

The scandal at David's palace did not end with his affair with Bathsheba and the subsequent death of their bastard son and Uriah, her husband and David's friend. Instead, the pattern of sexual sin and murder came to characterize the greater family relationships. The close connection between the father's sin and the son's subsequent behavior is clear—the story of Amnon and Absalom (2 Samuel 13-19) follows directly after the story of Bathsheba (2 Samuel 11-12). Like tabloid press coverage of the British monarchy, what unfolds is a detailed and graphic portrayal of moral corruption in the royal family.

The story in a nutshell follows: When Amnon, David's eldest son and heir apparent, rapes his beautiful half-sister Tamar, her brother Absalom (who is next in succession to the throne) burns within. Two years later he takes revenge on Amnon, hosting a party in his honor and then ordering his friends to put Amnon to death while he lies drunk.

Afterward, Absalom flees the country and is estranged from David for three years. Upon returning he orchestrates a coup to overthrow his father; a bloody civil war results. In the midst of the conflict Absalom is killed, even though David gave his military commanders strict orders not to harm his rebellious son.

Upon hearing of his son's death, David wept, exclaiming the most heartrending words of a parent: "O my son Absalom! My son, my son Absalom! If only I had died instead of you—O Absalom, my son, my son!" (2 Samuel 18:33).

David's anguish, like those of other parents, is unimaginable. I would guess that the thirty-eight parents of those who died at Columbine High School—Eric Harris and Dylan Klebold as well as Cassie Bernall and Rachel Scott—have uttered words similar to David's: "If only I had died instead of you."

But what about us? Are we willing to die for our teenage children? Would we take the blame or the bullet for our sons and daughters? I suspect that most of us would indeed make this ultimate sacrifice. Then we must pose the question at a more mundane level: Are we willing to make the incremental sacrifices that are necessary to have an influence in our teenager's life?

THE HEART OF GOD

God uses our children as tools to make our hearts like that of Jesus as He hung on the cross. He died that we might live, and so too must we for the sake of our children. We, however, often want to be like Jesus only in theory. We are not really willing to sacrifice our time, expectations, career, or control. But this is what is required.

"Self-giving, not self-fulfillment, lies at the heart of the parents' vocation," theologian Gilbert Meilaender reminds us. "If such a self-giving should prove to be deeply satisfying, we have reason to be thankful. But there are no guarantees of such symmetrically satisfying results, and to seek them is not the best preparation for parenthood."[1] We are to love without limits. We need to give without guarantees.

In the Bible we have not received a how-to book on no-fault

child-rearing. Instead, through it we are to become apprentices of Jesus, following Him and modeling His life and love in the significant relationships of our lives. Parents are to be "little Christs" within their homes.

God's intent is that we should learn to love like Jesus. In brutal simplicity, it falls out like this: No life, no love; no love, no life. True spirituality starts at home — in our marriages and with our children — and begins with the transformation of our hearts. Parenting starts with the parent.

There will never be the perfect family. But there can be parents whose desire is to love like Jesus, whatever it takes. It is an inside-out process for us and for our teenagers. As we allow God to break our hearts we will learn to love with real tears and open hands. Then we will cry from the heart, "If only I had died instead of you." This is the way of our Savior.

Notes

Introduction: No Guaranty, No Warranty
[1] David Runcorn, *A Center of Quiet: Hearing God When Life Is Noisy* (Downers Grove, Ill: InterVarsity, 1990), p. 85.
[2] Mary Motley Kalergis, *Seen and Heard: Teenagers Talk About Their Lives* (New York: Stewart, Tabori & Chang, 1998), p. 9.

Chapter 1: Empty Promises
[1] See Gregory Bodenhamer, *Parents in Control* (New York: Simon & Schuster, 1995).
[2] Quoted in Ethan Watters, "Straight, Inc.," *Spin*, May 1999, p. 136.
[3] Dallas Willard, *In Search of Guidance: Developing a Conversational Relationship with God* (New York: HarperSanFrancisco, 1993), p. 21.
[4] Dallas Willard, *The Divine Conspiracy: Rediscovering Our Hidden Life in God* (New York: HarperSanFrancisco, 1998), p. 230.
[5] Gordon D. Fee and Douglas Stuart, *How to Read the Bible for All Its Worth* (Grand Rapids, Mich.: Zondervan, 1993), p. 217.
[6] Edward Gross, as quoted by Denis Haack, "Legalism in a Decaying Culture," *Critique*, #1-1999, p. 2. See Edward N. Gross, *Will My Children Go to Heaven?: Hope and Help for Believing Parents* (Philadelphia: Presbyterian & Reformed, 1995).
[7] Tedd Tripp, *Shepherding a Child's Heart* (Wapwallopen, Pa.: Shepherd Press, 1995), p. 32.
[8] See Cynthia Ulrich Tobias's *"You Can't Make Me" [But I Can Be Persuaded]: Strategies for Bringing Out the Best in Your Strong-Willed Child* (Colorado Springs: WaterBrook Press, 1999).
[9] Judith Rich Harris, *The Nurture Assumption* (New York: Free Press, 1998), p. 351.

Chapter 2: Anxiety Epidemic
[1] Patricia Hersch, as quoted by Deirdre Donahue, "Struggling to Raise Good Kids in Toxic Times: Is Innocence Evaporating in an Open-Door Society?" *USA Today*, 1 October 1998, p. 1D.
[2] Bill McKibben, as quoted by Donahue, p. 2D.
[3] Donahue, p. 2D.

[4] Patricia Hersch, *A Tribe Apart: A Journey into the Heart of American Adolescence* (New York: Fawcett Columbine, 1998), p. 12.

[5] Mihaly Csikzentmihalyi and Reed Larson, as quoted by Hersch, p. 20.

[6] Hersch, p. 21.

[7] Lucy Smith, as quoted by Mary Motley Kalergis, *Seen and Heard: Teenagers Talk About Their Lives* (New York: Stewart, Tabori & Chang, 1998), p. 66.

[8] Hersch, p. 118.

[9] Hersch, p. 285.

[10] Dana Mack, *The Assault on Parenthood: How Our Culture Undermines the Family* (New York: Simon & Schuster, 1997).

[11] See Brian D. Ray, *Home Schooling on the Threshold: A Survey of Research at the Dawn of the New Millennium* (Salem, Ore.: National Home Education Research Institute, 1999). Available through the National Home Education Research Institute, P.O. Box 13939, Salem, OR 97309, (503) 364-1490, or www.nheri.org.

[12] Samuel Blumenfeld, *Homeschooling: A Parent's Guide to Teaching Children* (Secaucus, N.J.: Citadel Press, 1998), p. 8.

[13] Debra Bell, *The Ultimate Guide to Homeschooling* (Dallas: Word, 1997), p. 7.

[14] C. S. Lewis, *The Four Loves* (Orlando: Harcourt Brace Jovanovich, 1988), p. 76.

Chapter 3: From the Heart

[1] Philippe Ariés, *Centuries of Childhood: A Social History of Family Life* (New York: Vintage, 1962), p. 32. See also Joseph F. Kett, *Rites of Passage: Adolescence in America 1790 to the Present* (New York: Basic Books, 1977); John Demos, *Past, Present and Personal: The Family and the Life Course in American History* (New York: Oxford University Press, 1986); and Thomas Hine, *The Rise and Fall of the American Teenager* (New York: Avon Books, 1999).

[2] Cynthia Crossen, "Growing Up Goes On and On and On," *Wall Street Journal*, 24 March 1997, p. B1.

[3] Crossen, p. B1.

[4] Stephanie Coontz, *The Way We Really Are: Coming to Terms with America's Changing Families* (New York: Basic Books, 1997), p. 13.

[5] Coontz, pp. 14-15.

[6] Tedd Tripp, *Shepherding a Child's Heart* (Wapwallopen, Pa.: Shepherd Press, 1995), p. 233.

[7] C. S. Lewis, *The Four Loves* (Orlando: Harcourt Brace Jovanovich, 1988), p. 66.

[8] Judith Rich Harris, *The Nurture Assumption* (New York: Free Press, 1998), p. 318.

[9] This is the central point of Tedd Tripp's *Shepherding a Child's Heart*, which is based on Proverbs 4:23.

[10] Dallas Willard, *In Search of Guidance* (New York: HarperSanFrancisco, 1993), p. 220.

[11] Willard, *The Divine Conspiracy* (New York: HarperSanFrancisco, 1998), p. 142.

[12] See Matthew 10:37-39; Luke 18:29.

[13] See Deuteronomy 6:6-7; Proverbs 13:24; 22:6.

[14] See Psalm 51:5; 58:3.

[15] See 1 Timothy 3:4-5,14; Titus 1:9.

[16] See Ephesians 6:4; Colossians 3:21.

[17] See Exodus 20:12; Proverbs 6:20-23; Ephesians 6:1-4; Colossians 3:20.

[18] See Proverbs 4:14-15; 12:26; 13:20; 1 Corinthians 15:33.

[19] See Romans 1:30; 2 Timothy 3:1-5.

[20] See Exodus 34:6-7; Numbers 14:18-19; Deuteronomy 5:8.

Chapter 4: The Madman's Warning

[1] Will Dana, "Hot Mood: Confusion," *Rolling Stone*, 22 August 1996, p. 84.

[2] R.E.M., "Bittersweet Me," *New Adventures in Hi-Fi* (Warner Brothers, 1996).

[3] Smashing Pumpkins, "Zero," *Mellon Collie and the Infinite Sadness* (Virgin Records, 1995).

[4] Quoted in Diana Schaub, "On the Character of Generation X," *The Public Interest*, Fall 1999, p. 3.

5 Mardi Keyes, "Who Invented Adolescence?" reprinted from *Critique* by Ransom Fellowship, 1994. Available through Ransom Fellowship, 1150 West Center Street, Rochester, MN 55902.

6 Erich Heller, *The Importance of Nietzsche* (Chicago: Chicago University Press, 1988), p. 5.

7 Ludwig Feuerbach, *The Essence of Christianity* (New York: Harper, 1957), p. 15.

8 Van Riessen, *Nietzsche* (Philadelphia: Presbyterian & Reformed, 1960), p. 51.

9 Heller, p. 11.

10 Heller, p. 4.

11 Friedrich Nietzsche, *The Gay Science* (New York: Vintage, 1974), pp. 181-182.

12 Richard Tarnas, *The Passion of the Western Mind: Understanding the Ideas That Have Shaped Our World View* (New York: Ballentine Books, 1991), p. 319.

13 T. S. Eliot, *A Choice of Kipling's Verse* (London: Faber and Faber, 1989), p. 136.

14 Blaise Pascal, *Pensées* (New York: Random House, 1941), p. 29/77.

15 Pascal, p. 137/430. The goal of the Enlightenment was to maintain a realist faith while declaring disallegiance from the God who was that faith's object. In effect, it wanted to keep the story and kill the storyteller. It proved a vicious failure.

16 C. S. Lewis, *The Abolition of Man* (New York: Macmillan, 1947), p. 77.

17 A. J. P. Taylor, *From Sarajevo to Potsdam* (London: Harcourt, Brace & World, 1965), pp. 55-56.

18 John Dominic Crossan, quoted by J. Richard Middleton and Brian J. Walsh, *Truth Is Stranger Than It Used to Be: Biblical Faith in a Postmodern Age* (Downers Grove, Ill.: InterVarsity, 1995), p. 62.

19 Richard Rorty, *Contingency, Irony, and Solidarity* (New York: Cambridge University Press, 1989), p. 22.

20 Kristin Johnson, as quoted by Mary Motley Kalergis, *Seen and Heard: Teenagers Talk About Their Lives* (New York: Stewart, Tabori & Chang, 1998), p. 124.

21 Charles Darwin, as quoted by Philip Yancey, "Nietzsche Was Right," *Books & Culture*, January/February 1998, p. 15.

Chapter 5: The Stealth Factor

1 Jann Wenner, "The Same Old Crap from William Bennett," *Rolling Stone*, 23 January 1997, p. 4.

2 See the 23 January 1997 issue of *Rolling Stone*. Manson was also featured in the 15 October 1998 issue, this time for his glam-rock album, *Mechanical Animal*.

3 Marilyn Manson, "Columbine: Whose Fault Is It?" *Rolling Stone*, 24 June 1999, pp. 23-24.

4 Alfred Schutz, *The Structures of the Life-World* (Chicago: Northwestern University Press, 1973), p. 4.

5 Dallas Willard, *The Divine Conspiracy* (New York: HarperSanFrancisco, 1998), p. 306.

6 C. S. Lewis, "Christian Apologetics," in *God in the Dock: Essays on Theology and Ethic* (Grand Rapids, Mich.: Eerdmans, 1970), p. 93.

7 A. W. Tozer, *A Treasury of A. W. Tozer* (Grand Rapids, MI: Baker Books, 1980), p. 141.

8 J. Gresham Machen, "Christianity and Culture," an address delivered on September 20, 1912, at the opening of the 101st session of Princeton Theological Seminary. Reprinted in *What Is Christianity?* (Grand Rapids, Mich.: Eerdmans, 1951), p. 156.

9 David Bosworth, "Endangered Species: The Mall as Political Habitat," *Salmagundi*, Spring-Summer 1998, pp. 228-229.

10 C. S. Lewis, "On the Transmission of Christianity," in *God in the Dock*, p. 116.

11 Blaise Pascal, *Penseés* (New York: Random House, 1941), p. 138/430.

12 Erich Heller, *The Importance of Nietzsche* (Chicago: Chicago University Press, 1988), p. 5.

13 Douglas Coupland, *Life After God* (New York: Pocket Books, 1994), dustjacket.

14 See the 23 January 1997 issue of *Rolling Stone*.

15 Quoted on the Internet Web site, "Marilyn Manson WebRing."

16 Michael Josephson, as quoted by Patricia Hersch, *A Tribe Apart: A Journey into the Heart of American Adolescence* (New York: Fawcett Columbine, 1998), p. 101.

[17] Clarence Darrow, as quoted by Philip Yancey, "Dark Nature," *Books & Culture*, March /April 1998, p. 11.

Chapter 6: Hubris and Hedonism

[1] James Nolan, *The Therapeutic State* (New York: New York University Press, 1998), p. 3.

[2] For a historical study of this process, see James Collier's *The Rise of Selfishness in America* (New York: Oxford University Press, 1991) and Jackson Lears's *No Place of Grace: Antimodernism and the Transformation of American Culture 1880-1920* (New York: Pantheon Books, 1981).

[3] Philip Rieff, *The Triumph of the Therapeutic: Uses of Faith After Freud* (Chicago: Chicago University Press, 1987), p. 13.

[4] James B. Twitchell, *For Shame: The Loss of Common Decency in American Culture* (New York: St. Martin's Press, 1998), p. 136. See David Powlison, "How Shall We Cure Troubled Souls?" in *The Coming Evangelical Crisis,* ed. John H. Armstrong (Chicago: Moody, 1996), pp. 207-225.

[5] Nick Cassavetes, "Gina Gershon," *Interview,* July 1997, p. 68.

[6] Harvard economist David Rieff writes, "The market economy, now global in scale, is by its nature corrosive of all established hierarchies and certainties." Quoted by Thomas Frank and Matt Weiland, eds., *Commodify Your Dissent: The Business of Culture in the New Gilded Age* (New York: Norton, 1997), p. 272.

[7] Thomas Frank, "Why Johnny Can't Dissent," in Frank and Weiland, p. 34.

[8] Robert Bellah et. al., *The Habits of the Heart: Individualism and Commitment in American Life* (Berkeley: University of California Press, 1985), p. 47.

[9] See Michael F. Brown, *The Channeling Zone: American Spirituality in an Anxious Age* (Cambridge: Harvard University Press, 1997), p. 7.

[10] Jeremiah Creedon, "God with a Million Faces," *Utne Reader,* July/August 1998, p. 46.

[11] Tom Beaudoin, *Virtual Faith: The Irreverent Spiritual Quest of Generation X* (San Francisco: Jossey-Bass, 1998).

[12] Richard Cimino and Don Lattin, *Shopping for Faith: American Religion in the New Millennium* (San Francisco: Jossey-Bass, 1998), p. 38.

[13] Camille Paglia in "She Wants Her TV! He Wants His Book!" *Harper's Magazine,* March 1991, p. 48.

[14] See also Michael O'Brien's *A Landscape with Dragons: The Battle for Your Child's Mind* (San Francisco: Ignatius, 1998) for an extensive study of neopagan themes found in pop culture and children's literature, especially in Disney's animated films.

[15] Bob Morris, "Meditation and Decoration: Om for the Home," *New York Times,* 30 June 1998, p. F7. For example, see Denise Linn's *Altars: Bringing Sacred Shrines into Your Everyday Life* (New York: Ballantine Books, 1999).

[16] Pamela Fiori, "Star Struck," *Town & Country,* January 1999, p. 11.

[17] C. S. Lewis, *An Experiment in Criticism* (New York: Cambridge University Press, 1961), p. 68.

[18] Neale Donald Walsch, *Conversations with God: An Uncommon Dialogue* (New York: Putnam, 1995). See also J. Budziszewski, "Conversations with Himself," *National Review,* 23 March 1998, pp. 53-54 and Ken Myers, "Best-Selling Spirituality: American Cultural Change and the New Shape of Faith," (Charlottesville, Va.: Mars Hill Audio, 1999), audiocassette, (800) 331-6407.

[19] Ruth Shalit, "Quality Wings: Angels on Television, Angels in America," *New Republic,* 20, 27 July 1998, p. 28.

[20] Gilbert K. Chesterton, *Orthodoxy* (New York: Doubleday, 1959), p. 76.

[21] Erik Davis, "The God Squad: Pop Stars Search for the Spirit in the Material World," *Spin,* January 1999, p. 86.

[22] Chesterton, p. 77.

[23] Harvard clinical psychologist Richard Noll has demonstrated that self-deification is the cornerstone of Jungian psychoanalysis. See Richard Noll, *The Aryan Christ: The Secret Life of Carl Jung* (New York: Random House, 1997).

24 Jewel, "Who Will Save Your Soul," *Pieces of You* (Atlantic Records, 1994).
25 Chesterton, p. 76.
26 David Denby, *Great Books* (New York: Simon & Schuster, 1996), p. 373.

Chapter 7: World Without Boundaries
1 Richard Rorty, *Contingency, Irony, and Solidarity* (New York: Cambridge University Press, 1989), p. 3.
2 See Walter Truett Anderson's *Reality Isn't What It Used to Be* (San Francisco: Harper & Row, 1990).
3 Daniel Boorstin, *The Image: A Guide to Pseudo Events in America* (New York: Atheneum, 1964), p. 240.
4 Jean Baudrillard, "The Evil Demon of Images/Simulacra," in Thomas Dochery, ed., *Postmodernism: A Reader* (New York: Columbia University Press, 1993), p. 197.
5 Mark C. Taylor, *Hiding* (Chicago: Chicago University Press, 1997), p. 264. Also see Tony Jones's discussion of the film *The Matrix* (1999) in "Liberated by Reality," *Books & Culture*, September/October 1999, p. 27.
6 Ada Louise Huxtable, *The Unreal America: Architecture and Illusion* (New York: New Press, 1997), p. 2.
7 Leanne Payne, *The Healing Presence* (Westchester, Ill: Crossway Books, 1989), p. 74.
8 Frederich Nietzsche, "On Truth and Lie in an Extra-Moral Sense," in Walter Kaufmann, ed., *The Viking Portable Nietzsche* (New York: Viking, 1975), pp. 46-47.
9 See Walter Truett Anderson's edited book, *The Truth About the Truth* (New York: Putnam, 1995). For a helpful discussion of what is called in academic circles the "hermeneutics of suspicion," see Merold Westphal's *Suspicion & Faith: The Religious Uses of Modern Atheism* (Grand Rapids, Mich.: Eerdmans, 1993).
10 See Crystal Downing, "Richard Rorty for the Silver Screen," *Books & Culture*, September/October 1999, pp. 8-10.
11 Richard Rorty, "Solidarity or Objectivity?" in *Objectivity, Relativism, and Truth* (New York: Cambridge University Press, 1991), p. 33.
12 Richard J. Bernstein, "One Step Forward, Two Steps Backward: Richard Rorty on Liberal Democracy and Philosophy," *Political Theory*, November, 1987, pp. 538-563.
13 Alan Wolfe, *One Nation, After All* (New York: Viking, 1998), p. 82.
14 Robert Bellah, *The Good Society* (New York: Knopf, 1991), p. 44.
15 Rage Against The Machine, "Take the Power Back," *Rage Against The Machine* (Sony, 1992).
16 Michael Novak, "Awakening from Nihilism," *First Things*, August/September 1994, p. 20.
17 Tom Peters, "The Brand Called YOU," *Fast Company*, August-September 1997, p. 84.
18 Quoted in Daniel H. Pink, "The Brand Called URL," *Net Company*, Fall 1999, p. 32.
19 Michiko Kakutani, "When Fluidity Replaces Maturity," *New York Times*, 20 March 1995, p. C15.
20 Richard John Neuhaus, "Bill Clinton and the American Character," *First Things*, June/July 1999, p. 64.

Chapter 8: A Declaration of Independence
1 Patricia Hersch, *A Tribe Apart: A Journey into the Heart of American Adolescence* (New York: Fawcett Columbine, 1998), p. 57.
2 Charles McGrath, "Being 13: A Photo Album," *New York Times Magazine*, 17 May 1998, p. 30.
3 Hersch, p. 85.
4 Tom Beaudoin, *Virtual Faith: The Irreverent Spiritual Quest of Generation X* (San Francisco: Jossey-Bass, 1998), p. 140.
5 St. Augustine, *Confessions* (New York: Oxford University Press, 1991), p. 24.
6 Richard Rodriquez, as quoted by Lauren Greenfield, *Fast Forward: Growing Up in the Shadow of Hollywood* (New York: Knopf, 1997), p. 126.

[7] Levon, as quoted by Greenfield, p. 87.

[8] Hersch, p. 237.

[9] Greenfield, p. 101.

[10] See William Finnegan's list of adolescent tribes in *Cold New World: Growing Up in a Harder Country* (New York: Random House, 1998), p. 349. His list includes skaters, skins, rockers, ravers, rebels, heshers, punks, Goths, jocks, Rude Boys, hippies, preps, nerds, snowboarders, Sharps, Bloods, Crips, *Sureños, Norteños,* gangstas, Unity rappers, neo-Nazis, cheerleaders, Satanists, and anarchists.

[11] Malcolm Gladwell, "Annals of Style: The Coolhunt," *New Yorker,* 17 March 1997, p. 86.

[12] Judith Fitzgerald, *Building a Mystery: The Story of Sarah McLachlin & Lilith Fair* (New York: Quarry Press, 1997), p. 75.

[13] Sarah McLachlin, "Building a Mystery," *Surfacing* (Arista, 1997).

[14] Fitzgerald, p. 211.

[15] Ozzie, as quoted by Greenfield, p. 117.

[16] Hersch, p. 129.

[17] Andy Bernstein, Lockhart Steele, Larry Chasnoff, and Brian Celentano, *The Pharmer's Almanac: The Unofficial Guide to Phish* (Berkeley: Berkeley Boulevard, 1998), p. vii.

[18] Peach Friedman, as quoted by Mary Motley Kalergis, *Seen and Heard: Teenagers Talk About Their Lives* (New York: Stewart, Tabori & Chang, 1998), p. 102.

[19] Jeffrey Jensen Arnett, *Metalheads: Heavy Metal Music and Adolescent Alienation* (Boulder, Colo.: Westview Press, 1995), p. 145.

[20] Arnett, p. 17.

[21] Nelson George, *Hip Hop America* (New York: Viking, 1998), p. ix.

[22] Charles Aron, "What the White Boy Means When He Says 'Yo'," *Spin,* 1 November 1998, p. 114.

[23] David Wild, "The Year in Music," *Rolling Stone,* 21 January 1999, p. 52.

[24] Aron, p. 119.

[25] George, p. ix.

[26] Aron, p. 103.

[27] Christopher John Farley, "Hip-Hop Nation," *Time,* 8 February 1999, p. 57.

[28] George, p. 41.

[29] Farley, p. 56.

[30] Farley, p. 62.

[31] Hersch, pp. 81, 86, 90. The life and music of Grammy Award-winning hip-hop artist Lauryn Hill stands in stark contrast to this negative orientation.

[32] G-mo, as quoted by Greenfield, p. 111.

[33] Charles Gandee, "Life Among the Mall Rats," *Vogue,* July 1993, p. 199.

[34] Touré, "Foxy Brown," *Rolling Stone,* 24 December 1998, 7 January 1999, p. 74.

[35] Lauryn Hill, "Final Hour," *The Miseducation of Lauryn Hill* (Ruffhouse, 1998).

[36] James Davison Hunter, *The State of Disunion: 1996 Survey of American Political Culture,* vol. 1, Summary Report (The Post-Modernity Project, Charlottesville, Va.: University of Virginia, 1996), pp. 88, 91.

[37] Arnett, p. 127.

[38] See John Seel, "Meet Your Neighborhood Pagan," *Re:generation Quarterly,* Fall 1997, p. 18.

[39] George Barna, *Generation Next: What You Need to Know About Today's Youth* (Ventura, Calif.: Regal, 1995), p. 32.

[40] Hersch, p. 100.

[41] Hersch, p. 195.

[42] William J. Bennett, *The Index of Leading Cultural Indicators: American Society at the End of the Twentieth Century* (Colorado Springs: WaterBrook Press, 1999), pp. 129-155; Allison Adato, "The Secret Lives of Teens," *Life,* March 1999, pp. 38-48; and "One in 5 Teen-Agers Is Armed, a Survey Finds," *New York Times,* 14 August 1998, p. A19. Data is based on a 1997 Centers for Disease Control and Prevention survey of 16,262 teenagers in 151 schools nationwide and the 1999 National Household

Survey on Drug Abuse by the U.S. Department of Health and Human Services.
43 Barna, p. 98.
44 Greenfield, pp. 38, 49.
45 Adato, pp. 39, 40.
46 Peter Carlson, "Carlson's 10 Laws of Celebrity," *Washington Post Magazine*, 5 December 1993, p. 38.
47 Mijanou, as quoted by Greenfield, p. 65.

Chapter 9: Nihilism Chic
1 Steve Garber tells the story of students who kept their spiritual grounding during their university years. His is a book well worth putting into the hands of every Christian high-school senior. See Steve Garber, *The Fabric of Faithfulness: Weaving Together Belief & Behavior During the University Years* (Downers Grove, Ill.: InterVarsity, 1996). Also recommended is J. Budziszewski, *How to Stay Christian in College: An Interactive Guide to Keeping the Faith* (Colorado Springs: NavPress, 1999).
2 See Christina Rathbone's *On the Outside Looking In: A Year in an Inner-City High School* (New York: Atlantic Monthly Press, 1998).
3 Mark Steyn, "Comic Oprah," *National Review*, 23 March 1998, p. 31.
4 Quoted in James B. Twitchell, *For Shame: The Loss of Common Decency in American Culture* (New York: St. Martin's Press, 1998), p. 259.
5 James Collier, *The Rise of Selfishness in America* (New York: Oxford University Press, 1991), p. 168.
6 Twitchell, p. 16.
7 Nirvana, "Smells Like Teen Spirit," *Nevermind* (Geffen, 1991).
8 Patrick Brantlinger, *Bread & Circuses: Theories of Mass Culture as Social Decay* (Ithaca, N.Y.: Cornell University Press, 1983), p. 22.
9 Philip Rieff, *The Triumph of the Therapeutic: Uses of Faith After Freud* (Chicago: Chicago University Press, 1987), p. 234.
10 Twitchell, p. 53.
11 Rob Sheffield, "Rage Against the Latrines," *Rolling Stone*, 2 September 1999, p. 52.
12 Matt Hendricks, "Moshing and Looting," *Rolling Stone*, 2 September 1999, p. 55.
13 David Samuels, "Rock Is Dead: Sex, Drugs, and Raw Sewage at Woodstock 99," *Harper's Magazine*, November 1999, p. 82.
14 Erik Hedegaard, "Jerry Springer: Strippers Who Kill! Killers Who Strip! We Have Seen the Enemy and He's on Jerry Springer," *Rolling Stone*, 14 May 1998, p. 47.
15 Sissela Bok, *Mayhem: Violence as Public Entertainment* (Reading, Mass.: Addison-Wesley, 1998), p. 27.
16 "Teens Held in Rape of Sister," *Philadelphia Daily News*, 8 January 1999, p. A1.
17 Fyodor Dostoyevsky, as quoted by V. Borisov, *From Under the Rubble* (New York: Little, Brown, 1975), p. 202.
18 Randall Sullivan, "A Boy's Life," *Rolling Stone*, 1 October 1998, p. 50.
19 T. Trent Gegax and Sarah Van Boven, "Heroin High," *Newsweek*, 1 February 1999, p. 54.
20 Gegax and Van Boven, p. 54.
21 Arch Puddington, "Jock Shock," *Weekly Standard*, 11 August 1997, p. 33. Also see Bernard Lefkowitz, *Our Guys: The Glen Ridge Rape and the Secret Life of the Perfect Suburb* (Berkeley, Calif.: University of California Press, 1997).
22 Iver Peterson, "After Deaths, County Asks 'Why?': Permissiveness Is Blamed as Teenagers Are Arrested," *New York Times*, 20 July 1998, p. B1.
23 Robert J. Samuelson, "Enough Blame to Go Around," *Washington Post*, 3 May 1999, p. A25.
24 Peggy Noonan, "The Culture of Death," *Wall Street Journal*, 22 April 1999, p. A22.
25 Jon Pareles, "They're Rebels Without a Cause, and They Couldn't Care Less," *New York Times*, Arts & Leisure, Sunday, 16 July 1995, p. 23. The novel of *Kids'* scriptwriter Harmony Korine, *A Crack Up at the Race Riots* (New York: Doubleday,

1998), provides twenty suicide notes with blank signature spaces at the bottom. Suicide notes as a form letter, he explains, just in case one faces death with a writer's block.

[26] William Finnegan, *Cold New World: Growing Up in a Harder Country* (New York: Random House, 1998), p. 351.

Chapter 10: Followers First

[1] C. S. Lewis, *The Four Loves* (Orlando: Harcourt Brace Jovanovich, 1988), p. 43.

[2] This book is largely a footnote on the life and writings of Dallas Willard who, through his books *The Spirit of the Disciplines* (1988), *In Search of Guidance* (1993), and *The Divine Conspiracy* (1998), has pointed me to the reality of life in Jesus. Willard's work stands as the backdrop of all that I have to say on the subject of parenting and is highly recommended.

[3] Parker J. Palmer, *The Courage to Teach: Exploring the Inner Landscape of a Teacher's Life* (San Francisco: Jossey-Bass, 1998), p. 10.

[4] Steven Daly, "Tori Amos: Her Secret Garden," *Rolling Stone*, 25 June 1998, p. 103.

[5] Jacqueline L. Salmon, "Children Under Surveillance: When Parents' Trust Wears Out, Some Resort to Spying on Their Teens," *Washington Post*, Sunday, 28 February 1999, pp. A1, A18.

[6] Gregory Bodenhamer, *Parents in Control* (New York: Simon & Schuster, 1995).

[7] E. Stanley Jones, as quoted by Dallas Willard, *In Search of Guidance* (New York: HarperSanFrancisco, 1993), p. 17; from E. Stanley Jones, *Victorious Living* (Nashville: Abingdon, 1938), p. 281.

[8] William Wilberforce, *Real Christianity* (Portland, Ore.: Multnomah, 1829/1982), pp. 58, 67.

[9] C. S. Lewis, "On the Transmission of Christianity," in *God in the Dock* (Grand Rapids, Mich.: Eerdmans, 1970), p. 116.

[10] Oswald Chambers, *My Utmost for His Highest* (New York: Dodd, Mead, 1935), p. 196.

[11] Dallas Willard, *The Divine Conspiracy* (New York: HarperSanFrancisco, 1998), p. 55.

[12] Willard, *The Divine Conspiracy*, p. 49.

[13] See Albert Hsu, "What Would Jesus Do About 'WWJD'?" *Re:generation Quarterly*, Winter 1998, pp. 6-7. "The WWJD phenomenon encourages a behavioristic approach to Christian life, where we become primarily concerned with outward decision-making, not the inward development of Christian character. It assumes that in the face of a moral decision, the totality of Christian discipleship is merely to *do* what Jesus would do—regardless of whether or not appropriate Christian motivation, attitude, or thinking is present."

[14] Willard, *The Divine Conspiracy*, p. 283.

[15] King James Version as paraphrased, *The Divine Conspiracy*, by Dallas Willard, p. 296.

[16] Willard, *The Divine Conspiracy*, p. 364.

[17] Daly, p. 103.

Chapter 11: "The Whole World Is Watching"

[1] Dick Keyes, *True Heroism in a World of Celebrity Counterfeits* (Colorado Springs: NavPress, 1995), p. 223.

[2] Dallas Willard, *The Divine Conspiracy* (New York: HarperSanFrancisco, 1998), p. 386.

[3] Neil Postman, "Learning by Story," *Atlantic Monthly*, December 1998, p. 122.

[4] Keyes, p. 224.

[5] Peter Kreeft, *Three Philosophies of Life* (San Francisco: Ignatius, 1989), p. 20.

[6] Quoted in Jon Spayde, "Learning in the Key of Life," *Utne Reader*, May-June 1998, p. 47.

[7] I am indebted to Peter Kreeft's *Three Philosophies of Life* for the basis of these observations.

[8] Jeffrey Jensen Arnett, *Metalheads: Heavy Metal Music and Adolescent Alienation* (Boulder, Colo.: Westview Press, 1995), p. 16.

[9] Chris Niles, "Wall Street Fighters," *The Times Magazine* (London), 7 August 1999, p. 44.

10 Søren Kierkegaard, as quoted by Kreeft, p. 41.
11 Philip P. Pan and Micahel E. Ruane, "Murder Suspect, 14, Lived in a World of Easy Guns," *Washington Post*, Sunday, 7 March 1999, p. C8.
12 As quoted by Lauren Greenfield, *Fast Forward: Growing Up in the Shadow of Hollywood* (New York: Knopf, 1997), p. 101.
13 Albert Camus, tr. Stuart Gilbert, *The Plague* (New York: Vintage, 1972), p. 154.
14 Postman, p. 124.
15 Chester E. Finn, Jr. and Bruno V. Manno, "Behind the Curtain," *Wilson Quarterly*, Winter 1996, p. 44.
16 See David Damrosch, *We Scholars: Changing the Culture of the University* (Cambridge: Harvard University Press, 1996).
17 Richard Rorty, *Essays on Heidegger and Others* (New York: Cambridge University Press, 1991), p. 86.
18 Kreeft, p. 21.
19 W. Somerset Maugham, *A Writer's Notebook* (New York: Doubleday, 1949), pp. 347-348.
20 Blaise Pascal, *The Mind on Fire* (Portland, Ore.: Multnomah, 1989), p. 229.
21 Jean-Paul Sartre, "Existentialism," in Lawrence Cahoone, *From Modernism to Postmodernism: An Anthology* (Malden, Mass.: Blackwell, 1997), p. 262.
22 Keyes, p. 225.
23 David John Seel, *Does My Father Know I'm Hurt?* (Wheaton, Ill.: Tyndale, 1971), p. 23.
24 See Acts 26:19.

Chapter 12: Going Native
1 Garry Wills, *Certain Trumpets: The Call of Leaders* (New York: Simon & Schuster, 1994), pp. 16, 17.
2 Wills, p. 21.
3 Parker J. Palmer, *Let Your Life Speak: Listening for the Voice of Vocation* (San Francisco: Jossey-Bass, 1999), p. 76.
4 Howard Gardner, *Leading Minds: An Anatomy of Leadership* (New York: Basic Books, 1995), p. 14.
5 Dallas Willard, *The Divine Conspiracy* (New York: HarperSanFrancisco, 1998), p. 308.
6 Sydney Lewis, *"a totally alien life-form"—teenagers* (New York: New Press, 1996), p. 13.
7 Paul David Tripp, *Age of Opportunity: A Biblical Guide to Parenting Teens* (Philadelphia: Presbyterian & Reformed, 1997), p. 80.
8 Willard, p. 217. See Chapter 7, "The Community of Prayerful Love," which establishes the biblical rationale for loving versus judging in human relationships.
9 Patricia Hersch, *A Tribe Apart: A Journey into the Heart of American Adolescence* (New York: Fawcett Columbine, 1998), p. 23.
10 Cristina Rathbone, *On the Outside Looking In: A Year in an Inner-City High School* (New York: Atlantic Monthly Press, 1998), p. 382.
11 Maureen Callahan, "Forever Young," *Spin*, February 1999, p. 64. For a list and brief description of fifty years of teen films, see "A Blizzard of White Panties" in the same issue, pp. 68-72.
12 Sarah McLachlan, "Dear God," *Coalition of Independent Music Stores Sampler* (Arista, 1997).
13 Indigo Girls, "Closer to Fine," *Indigo Girls* (CBS, 1989).
14 Willard, *In Search of Guidance* (New York: HarperSanFrancisco, 1993), p. 79.
15 Willard, *In Search of Guidance*, p. 46.

Chapter 13: "Proud Parent of a Skateboarder"
1 Nicholas Evans, *The Loop* (New York: Delacorte, 1998), pp. 98, 99, 100.
2 Alanis Morissette, "Perfect," *jagged little pill* (Maverick, 1995).
3 Tori Amos, "Girl," *Little Earthquakes* (Atlantic, 1991).

4 J. I. Packer, *A Quest for Godliness: The Puritan Vision of the Christian Life* (Wheaton, Ill.: Crossway, 1990), p. 22. See also Peter Lewis, *The Genius of Puritanism* (Hayward Heath, England: Carey Publications, 1979).

5 Adapted from William Perkins' excerpt in Edmund S. Morgan, ed., *Puritan Political Ideas: 1558-1794* (Indianapolis, Ind.: Bobbs-Merrill, 1965), pp. 51-59.

6 Frederick Buechner, *Wishful Thinking—A Seeker's ABC* (New York: HarperCollins, 1993), pp. 118-119.

7 See Paul Marshall's *Heaven Is Not My Home: Living in the Now of God's Creation* (Nashville: Word, 1998) and Michael S. Horton's *Where In the World Is the Church?: A Christian View of Culture and Your Role in It* (Grand Rapids, Mich.: Baker, 1995).

8 C. S. Lewis, *Surprised by Joy* (New York: Harcourt, Brace and Company, 1955), p. 183.

9 Lewis, p. 184.

10 Dick Keyes, *True Heroism in a World of Celebrity Counterfeits* (Colorado Springs: NavPress, 1995), p. 226.

Chapter 14: Reality Bites

1 Max Weber, *Economy and Society: An Outline of Interpretive Sociology* (Berkeley: University of California Press, 1978), pp. 212-298.

2 W. Somerset Maugham, *The Summing Up* (New York: Penguin, 1963), p. 179.

3 James L. Nolan, *The Therapeutic State* (New York: New York University Press, 1998), p. 285.

4 C. S. Lewis, "The Poison of Subjectivism," in *Christian Reflections* (Grand Rapids, Mich.: Eerdmans, 1994), p. 73.

5 Michael D. Aeschliman, *C. S. Lewis and the Case Against Scientism* (Grand Rapids, Mich.: Eerdmans, 1983), p. 76.

6 Mark Dery, *Escape Velocity: Cyberculture at the End of the Century* (New York: Grove Press, 1996), p. 302. See also Keith Ansell Pearson's *Viroid Life: Perspectives on Nietzsche and the Transhuman Condition* (New York: Routledge, 1997) and Erik Davis, *TechGnosis: Myth, Magic, and Mysticism in the Age of Information* (New York: Harmony Press, 1998).

7 Dery, p. 294.

8 Derek Freeman, *Margaret Mead and Samoa: The Making and Unmaking of an Anthropological Myth* (Cambridge: Harvard University Press, 1983). Philosopher J. Budziszewski writes that a common approach used in the academy to disconnect traditional morality from human nature is to promote a "false anthropology, whereby young people are taught the wholly spurious idea that the human race is in complete disagreement about all the elementary points of right and wrong." See his *Written on the Heart: The Case for Natural Law* (Downers Grove, Ill.: InterVarsity, 1997), p. 174, as well as Michael Cromartie, ed., *A Preserving Grace: Protestants, Catholics, and Natural Law* (Grand Rapids, Mich.: Eerdmans, 1997).

9 C. S. Lewis, "On Ethics" in *Christian Reflections*, pp. 46, 55.

10 C. S. Lewis, *The Abolition of Man* (New York: Macmillan, 1971), p. 58.

11 Kreeft, p. 43.

12 Augustine, *Confessions* (New York: Oxford University Press, 1991), p. 145.

13 E. Michael Jones, *Degenerate Moderns: Modernity as Rationalized Sexual Misbehavior* (San Francisco: Ignatius, 1993), pp. 252, 253.

14 Jones, p. 16.

15 Friedrich Nietzsche, *Beyond Good and Evil* (New York: Vintage, 1966), p. 13.

16 See, for example, James Miller's *The Passion of Michel Foucault* (New York: Simon & Schuster, 1993). Here is the biography of a true postwar Nietzschean, a leading exemplar of the deathwork culture. Foucault wrote, "The key to the personal poetic attitude of a philosopher is not to be sought in his ideas, as if it could be deduced from them, but rather in his philosophy-as-life, in his philosophical life, his ethos" (p. 9).

[17] Peter Kreeft and Ronald K. Tacelli, *Handbook of Christian Apologetics* (Downers Grove, Ill.: InterVarsity, 1994), p. 382.

[18] George Orwell, as quoted by J. Budziszewski, *Written on the Heart: The Case for Natural Law* (Downers Grove, Ill.: InterVarsity, 1997), p. 171. A scholarly study of the natural-law tradition, Budziszewski's brief chapter "The Art of Teaching," is well worth reading.

[19] See Sissela Bok, *Mayhem: Violence as Public Entertainment* (Reading, Mass.: Addison-Wesley, 1998).

[20] Leo Tolstoy, *A Calendar of Wisdom* (New York: Scribner, 1997), p. 226.

[21] C.S. Lewis, as quoted in Kreeft and Tacelli, p. 363.

[22] David F. Wells, *Losing Our Virtue: Why the Church Must Recover Its Moral Vision,* (Grand Rapids, Mich.: Eerdmans, 1998), p. 163.

[23] Charles Peirce, quoted in Susan Haack, *Manifesto of a Passionate Moderate: Unfashionable Essays* (Chicago: University of Chicago Press, 1998), p. 32.

[24] C. S. Lewis, *Surprised by Joy* (New York: Harcourt, Brace and Company, 1955), p. 177.

[25] Agnes Sanford, *The Healing Gifts of the Spirit* (New York: Harper & Row, 1966), p. 25.

[26] Pascal, p. 153/464.

[27] Lewis, *The Weight of Glory,* p. 2.

[28] Lewis, *The Weight of Glory,* p. 5.

[29] Lewis, *The Pilgrim's Regress,* p. 123.

[30] Leanne Payne, *Real Presence: The Christian Worldview of C. S. Lewis as Incarnational Reality* (Wheaton, Ill.: Crossway Books, 1988), p. 32.

[31] Augustine, as quoted by Mary W. Tileston, *Great Souls at Prayer* (Cambridge, England: James Clark & Company, 1980), p. 108.

Chapter 15: "Whatever"

[1] Gilbert K. Chesterton, *Orthodoxy* (New York: Doubleday, 1959), p. 84.

[2] Miguel de Unamuno, "Saint Emmanuel the Good, Martyr," in Frederick R. Karl and Leo Hamalian, eds., *The Existential Imagination* (New York: Fawcett, 1963), pp. 103, 106.

[3] Unamuno, p. 129.

[4] Dorothy Sayers, as quoted by *Moral Compasses for Modern Leaders: The Cardinal Virtues and Deadly Vices in Everyday Life* (Burke, Va.: The Trinity Forum, 1996), pp. 3-13.

[5] Tom Beaudoin, *Virtual Faith: The Irreverent Spiritual Quest of Generation X* (San Francisco: Jossey-Bass, 1998), p. 13.

[6] C. S. Lewis, "Revival or Decay," in *God in the Dock* (Grand Rapids, Mich.: Eerdmans, 1970), pp. 250-251.

[7] William Wilberforce, *Real Christianity: Contrasted with the Prevailing Religious System* (Portland, Ore.: Multnomah, 1829/1982), pp. 127-128.

[8] Blaise Pascal, *Pensées* (New York: Random House, 1941), p. 91/260.

[9] Václav Havel, *Letters to Olga* (New York: Knopf, 1988), p. 237.

[10] Pascal, p. 92/261.

[11] Peter Kreeft, *Christianity for Modern Pagans* (San Francisco: Ignatius, 1998), p. 211.

[12] As quoted in "Money, Not Learning, Is Freshman's Top Goal," *USA Today,* 21 January 1998, p. D1.

[13] Kreeft, p. 253.

[14] Pascal, p. 190/580.

[15] Mark 4:11-12; also Matthew 13:11-15.

[16] Luke 5:14; see also Mark 3:12, 5:43, and 7:36.

[17] Pascal, p. 91/259.

[18] Paraphrased from Thomas C. Oden, ed., *Parables of Kierkegaard* (Princeton, N.J.: Princeton University Press, 1978), pp. 40-41.

[19] Søren Kierkegaard, as quoted by Oden, p. 45.

[20] Kreeft, p. 246.

[21] Pascal, p. 140/430.

[22] Chesterton, *What's Wrong with the World* (Peru, Ill.: Sherwood Sugden & Company, 1910), p. 29.

[23] Kreeft, p. 217.

[24] Dallas Willard, *The Divine Conspiracy* (New York: HarperSanFrancisco, 1998), p. 307. See also J. P. Moreland, "Beliefs, Behavior, and Character," in *Love Your God with All Your Mind* (Colorado Springs: NavPress, 1997), pp. 73-77. Moreland writes, "Beliefs are the rails upon which our lives run. We almost always act according to what we really believe. It doesn't matter much what we say we believe or what others think we believe. When the rubber meets the road, we act out our actual beliefs most of the time. That is why behavior is such a good indicator of a person's beliefs."

[25] Willard, p. 307.

[26] Wilberforce, p. 2.

[27] Wilberforce, p. 4.

[28] C. S. Lewis, *Mere Christianity* (New York: Macmillan, 1952), p. 75.

Chapter 16: The Lock and Key

[1] See J. P. Moreland's "The Minds Role in Spiritual Transformation" in *Love Your God with All Your Mind: The Role of Reason in the Life of the Soul* (Colorado Springs: NavPress, 1997).

[2] Patricia Hersch, *A Tribe Apart: A Journey into the Heart of American Adolescence* (New York: Fawcett Columbine, 1998), p. 365.

[3] Dick Keyes, *True Heroism in a World of Celebrity Counterfeits* (Colorado Springs: NavPress, 1995), p. 225.

[4] Dallas Willard, *The Spirit of the Disciplines* (New York: Harper & Row, 1988), p. 180.

[5] See Thomas Cahill, *How the Irish Saved Civilization* (New York: Doubleday, 1995).

[6] Dallas Willard, *The Divine Conspiracy* (New York: HarperSanFrancisco, 1998), p. 225. See his entire discussion on condemnation and how to avoid "managing" others, pp. 217-234.

[7] Bertrand Russell, *What I Believe* (New York: Dutton, 1929), p. 116.

[8] C. S. Lewis, "Man or Rabbit?" in *God in the Dock* (Grand Rapids, Mich.: Eerdmans, 1970), p. 108.

[9] Willard, *The Divine Conspiracy*, pp. 93-95. He writes, "This confidence in his intellectual greatness is the basis of the radicalism of Christ-following in relation to the human order. . . . 'Jesus is Lord' can mean little in practice for anyone who has to hesitate before saying, 'Jesus is smart.'"

[10] Gilbert K. Chesterton, *Orthodoxy* (New York: Doubleday, 1959), p. 75.

[11] Blaise Pascal, *Pensées* (New York: Random House, 1941), pp. 95, 96/282.

[12] Pascal, p. 95/277.

[13] Pascal, p. 94/273.

[14] Peter Kreeft, *Christianity for Modern Pagans* (San Francisco: Ignatius, 1993), p. 238.

[15] Francis Schaeffer, *The God Who Is There* (Downers Grove, Ill.: InterVarsity, 1968), p. 129.

[16] Friedrich Nietzsche, *The Gay Science* (New York: Vintage, 1974), p. 283.

[17] Pascal, as quoted by Kreeft, p. 325.

[18] Simon Reynolds, *Generation Ecstasy: Into the World of Techno and Rave Culture* (New York: Little, Brown, 1998), pp. 208-209.

[19] Quoted in George Sayer, *Jack: A Life of C. S. Lewis* (Wheaton, Ill.: Crossway Books, 1994), p. 86.

[20] C. S. Lewis, *Surprised by Joy* (New York: Harcourt, Brace and Company, 1955), p. 175.

[21] In Louise Cowan and Os Guinness, eds., "The Importance of the Classics," *Invitation to the Classics: A Guide to Books You've Always Wanted to Read* (Grand Rapids, Mich.: Baker, 1998), p. 20.

[22] See also William Kilpatrick and Gregory and Suzanne M. Wolfe, *Books That Build Character: A Guide to Teaching Moral Values Through Stories* (New York: Touchstone, 1994) and Terry W. Glaspey, *Great Books of the Christian Tradition* (Eugene, Ore.:

Harvest House, 1996), as well as the following three resources: A Common Reader: Books for Readers with Imagination, (800) 832-7323; Eighth Day Books: A Unique Collection of Classics in Religion, Philosophy, History, and Literature, (800) 841-2541; and God's World Book Club, (800) 951-BOOK.

23 Richard J. Foster, *The Celebration of Discipline* (New York: HarperSanFrancisco, 1998), p. 1.
24 Augustine, *Confessions* (New York: Oxford University Press, 1991), p. 51.
25 Chesterton, p. 84.
26 Wolterstorff, p. 59.
27 Wolterstorff, p. 61.
28 Peter Kreeft, *The Journey: A Spiritual Roadmap for Modern Pilgrims* (Downers Grove, Ill.: InterVarsity, 1996); James W. Sire, *The Universe Next Door: A Basic Worldview Catalog* (Downers Grove, Ill.: InterVarsity, 1997); and *The Journey: A Thinking Leader's Quest for Spiritual Meaning* (Burke, Va.: The Trinity Forum, 1995), available from The Trinity Forum, 7902 Westpark Drive, Suite A, McLean, VA 22102-4202, (800) 585-1070.
29 Kreeft, *The Journey*, pp. 9-10.
30 James W. Sire, *The Universe Next Door: A Basic Worldview Catalog* (Downers Grove, Ill.: InterVarsity, 1997), p. 18.

Chapter 17: Out of Control
1 In Roger Steer, *J. Hudson Taylor: A Man in Christ* (Singapore: OMF Books, 1990), pp. 46-47.
2 Quoted in Steer, p. 209.
3 Henri J. M. Nouwen, *The Return of the Prodigal Son: A Story of Homecoming* (New York: Continuum, 1995), p. 40.
4 Nouwen, p. 33.
5 Nouwen, p. 90.
6 Dick Keyes, *True Heroism in a World of Celebrity Counterfeits* (Colorado Springs: NavPress, 1995), p. 228.
7 See David Gutmann, "The Paternal Imperative," *American Scholar,* Winter 1998, p. 120.
8 C. S. Lewis, *The Four Loves* (Orlando: Harcourt Brace Jovanovich, 1988), p. 51.
9 Sarah Parnell, as quoted by Mary Motley Kalergis, *Seen and Heard: Teenagers Talk About Their Lives* (New York: Stewart, Tabori & Chang, 1998), p. 76.
10 In Kalergis, p. 10.
11 Paul David Tripp, *Age of Opportunity: A Biblical Guide to Parenting Teens* (Philadelphia: Presbyterian & Reformed, 1997), pp. 36-37. Ranald Macauley and Jerram Barrs write in *Being Human: The Nature of Spiritual Experience* (Downers Grove, Ill.: InterVarsity, 1978), p. 184, "The independence of the child should be the goal to which parents aim. And it should be fostered deliberately so that with each succeeding year, quietly and perhaps imperceptibly because of its gradualness, the child moves from being under the parents to being alongside them."
12 Dallas Willard, *The Divine Conspiracy* (New York: HarperSanFrancisco, 1998), p. 229.
13 Keyes, p. 228.
14 J. P. Moreland, *Love Your God with All Your Mind: The Role of Reason in the Life of the Soul* (Colorado Springs: NavPress, 1997), p. 98.
15 Luigi Giussani, *The Religious Sense* (Montreal: McGill-Queen's University Press, 1997), p. 9.
16 Giussani, p. 9.
17 C. S. Lewis, *The Great Divorce* (New York: Macmillan, 1974), p. 72.
18 Tripp, p. 35.
19 Patricia Hersch, *A Tribe Apart: A Journey into the Heart of American Adolescence* (New York: Fawcett Columbine, 1998), pp. 71, 237.
20 As quoted by Jeffrey Jensen Arnett, *Metalheads: Heavy Metal Music and Adolescent Alienation* (Boulder, Colo.: Westview Press, 1995), p. 144.

21 Judith Rich Harris, *The Nurture Assumption* (New York: Free Press, 1998), p. 241.

22 Willard, p. 228.

23 Maria Glod, "Public School Fills in the Gaps, Says Home-Taught Teen," *Washington Post,* Sunday, 15 November 1998, p. B5.

Chapter 18: The Divine Majority

1 In John Hollander, ed., *American Poetry: The Nineteen Century, Volume 2: Melville to Stickney* (New York: Library of America, 1993), p. 241.

2 Judith Farr, *The Passion of Emily Dickinson* (Cambridge: Harvard University Press, 1997), p. 85.

3 Judith Rich Harris, *The Nurture Assumption* (New York: Free Press, 1998), p. 133.

4 C. S. Lewis, *The Four Loves* (Orlando: Harcourt Brace Jovanovich, 1988), p. 80.

5 Dallas Willard, *In Search of Guidance* (New York: HarperSanFrancisco, 1993), p. 82.

6 For an overview, see Malcolm Gladwell, "Annals of Behavior: Do Parents Matter?" *New Yorker,* 17 August 1998, pp. 54-64 and Margaret G. Alter, "Do Parents Matter?" *Books & Culture,* March/April 1999, pp. 26-27. Both authors give favorable reviews of Harris's book and both reviewers are Christians.

7 Harris received the highest award given by the American Psychological Association in 1998 for her research that led to her book, *The Nurture Assumption,* which has been itself selected as a Finalist for the Pulitzer Prize in Nonfiction in 1999.

8 Harris, p. 264.

9 Harris, p. 147.

10 Harris, p. 198.

11 Margaret G. Alter, "Do Parents Matter?" *Books & Culture,* March/April 1999, p. 26.

12 James S. Coleman et. al., *Equality of Educational Opportunity* (New York: Arno, 1979), p. 183.

13 Arthur G. Powell, *Lessons from Privilege: The American Prep School Tradition* (Cambridge: Harvard University Press, 1996), p. 37.

14 Ralph Waldo Emerson, as quoted by Powell, p. 46.

15 Patricia Hersch, *A Tribe Apart: A Journey into the Heart of American Adolescence* (New York: Fawcett Columbine, 1998), pp. 237, 255.

16 Gregory Bodenhamer, *Parents in Control* (New York: Simon & Schuster, 1995), p. 164.

17 Lewis, p. 80.

18 Obviously, if the educational choice is a public school, then the two decisions are usually the same.

19 Harris, p. 78.

20 Harris, p. 211.

21 Harris, p. 216.

22 C. S. Lewis, *The Letters of C. S. Lewis to Arthur Greeves* (New York: Macmillan, 1986), p. 477.

23 Harris, p. 253.

24 Robert J. Samuelson, "Enough Blame to Go Around," *Washington Post,* 3 May 1999, p. A25.

25 Lucy Smith, as quoted by Mary Motley Kalergis, *Seen and Heard:Teenagers Talk About Their Lives* (New York: Stewart, Tabori & Chang, 1998), p. 66.

26 Keith Harris, as quoted by Kalergis, p. 47.

27 Matt Labash, "'Do You Believe in God?' 'Yes.'," *Weekly Standard,* 10 May 1999, p. 23.

Chapter 19: For Our Child, Like a Child

1 Quoted in Roger Pooley and Philip Seddon, eds., *The Lord of the Journey: A Reader in Christian Spirituality* (San Francisco: HarperCollins, 1986), p. 225.

2 Quoted in Dr. and Mrs. Howard Taylor, *Hudson Taylor's Spiritual Secrets* (Chicago: Moody, 1989), p. 182.

3 Quoted in Pooley and Seddon, p. 216.

[4] Quoted in Dr. and Mrs. Howard Taylor, p. 124.
[5] Dallas Willard, *The Divine Conspiracy* (New York: HarperSanFrancisco, 1998), pp. 244, 246.
[6] Taylor, p. 152.
[7] Taylor, p. 120.
[8] Taylor, p. 78.
[9] Richard Foster, *Prayer: Finding the Heart's True Home* (New York: HarperSanFrancisco, 1992), p. 196.
[10] Taylor, p. 32.
[11] Taylor, p. 186.
[12] Taylor, pp. 166-167.
[13] Oswald Chambers, *My Utmost for His Highest* (New York: Dodd, Mead, 1935), p. 47.
[14] Taylor, p. 102.
[15] Taylor, p. 187.
[16] Foster, p. 196.

Conclusion: "Absalom! Absalom!"
[1] Gilbert Meilaender, "What Are Families For," *First Things,* October 1990, p. 116.

About the Author

JOHN SEEL is an educator and cultural analyst. He is the Headmaster of Logos Academy, a Christ-centered classical college preparatory school in Dallas, Texas.

The son of Presbyterian medical missionaries, he was raised in Chonju, Korea. An avid outdoorsman and certified Wilderness Emergency Medical Technician, he has climbed numerous peaks in the French Alps and Northern Cascades. He is married to Kathryn, a professional SCUBA diver, and has three children, Annie, David, and Alex.

John has a B.A. from Austin College, an M.Div. from Covenant Theological Seminary, and a Ph.D. from the University of Maryland (College Park). He taught at The Stony Brook School, a college preparatory school on Long Island, New York, and has served as a Senior Fellow at The Trinity Forum and the Institute for Advanced Studies in Culture at the University of Virginia. He is author of *The Evangelical Forfeit* (Baker 1993) and coeditor of *No God But God: Breaking with the Idols of Our Age* (Moody 1992).

MORE HELP FOR RAISING GREAT KIDS.

Raising Adults

Are your children becoming adults, or just adult-aged children?
Jim Hancock challenges assumptions and creates common
ground giving you the tools that teach children to accept responsibility and gain an adult perspective on life.
Raising Adults (Jim Hancock) $11

Becoming the Parent God Wants You to Be

Written by best-selling author Dr. Kevin Leman, *Becoming the
Parent God Wants You to Be* is a real-life parenting curriculum
that helps you discover you can be a great parent--without being
perfect!
Becoming the Parent God Wants You to Be
(Dr. Kevin Leman) $12

Parenting with Love and Logic

Need help with your kids? Learn how to parent kids of all ages
with love and logic and be amazed at the great results.
Parenting with Love and Logic
(Foster Cline & Jim Fay) $18

Get your copies today at your local bookstore, through our website at
www.navpress.com, or by calling (800) 366-7788.
Ask for offer **#6056** or a FREE catalog of NavPress resources.

NAVPRESS
BRINGING TRUTH TO LIFE
www.navpress.com

Prices subject to change.